After Wittgenstein,
St. Thomas

Other Titles of Interest from St. Augustine's Press

AFTER WITTGENSTEIN, ST. THOMAS

Roger Pouivet

Translated and introduced by
Michael S. Sherwin, O.P.

ST. AUGUSTINE'S PRESS
South Bend, Indiana
2006

Originally published as *Après Wittgenstein, Saint Thomas*
© Presses Universitaires de France, 1997

Manufactured in the United States of America.

1 2 3 4 5 6   13 12 11 10 09 08

Library of Congress Cataloging in Publication Data.
Pouivet, Roger, 1958–
[Après Wittgenstein, saint Thomas. English]
After Wittgenstein, Saint Thomas / by Roger Pouivet;
translated and introduced by Michael S. Sherwin. –
1st English ed.
p. cm.
Includes bibliographical references and index.
ISBN 1-58731-015-5 (hardcover: alk. paper)
1. Wittgenstein, Ludwig, 1889–1951. 2. Thomas, Aquinas,
Saint, 1225?–1274. I. Sherwin, Michael S., 1963– II. Title.
B3376.W564P6513 2005
192–dc22   2005005590

∞ *The paper used in this publication meets the minimum requirements of
the International Organisation for Standardization (ISO) – Paper for doc-
uments – Requirements for permanence – ISO 9706: 1994.*

St. Augustine's Press
www.staugustine.net

For
Hélène,
Clément
and Tomasz

Contents

TRANSLATOR'S INTRODUCTION

Roger Pouivet has written a challenging book. He advances views that both students of Aquinas and of Wittgenstein will find objectionable. In spite of this, or perhaps partly because of it, his slender volume merits close attention. Pouivet has with great economy articulated an often-overlooked fact: the work of the later Wittgenstein can help us discern the lasting value of Thomas Aquinas' philosophical anthropology. At the same time, Pouivet shows that Aquinas can help the reader avoid an influential misreading of Wittgenstein. In presenting this twofold argument, Pouivet pushes the reader to consider the extent to which his or her own understanding of the human person remains haunted by a lingering Cartesian dualism.

In his opening remarks, Pouivet alerts the reader that his interpretation of Wittgenstein is shaped by the work of three British philosophers: Elizabeth Anscombe, Peter Geach, and Anthony Kenny. Pouivet's study, however, is not so much an introduction to their thought, as a creative engagement with it. He chooses elements from within their works and suggests that they belong to a common set of concerns. He describes these concerns as constituting a perspective he provocatively calls *Wittgensteinian Thomism*. All three would probably object to being called either Wittgensteinians or Thomists. Throughout their careers they eschewed schools and labels, seeing themselves first and foremost as working philosophers. Nonetheless, the title is apt. They were all deeply influenced by both Wittgenstein and St. Thomas, and were aware of the affinities existing between these two great thinkers.

Elizabeth Anscombe (1919–2001) was arguably the greatest philosopher of the three. As a student at Oxford she both converted to Catholicism and married her fellow Catholic convert and philosopher, Peter Geach, with whom she raised seven children over their almost sixty years of married life. It was during her post-graduate studies at Cambridge in the early 1940s that she began to attend Wittgenstein's lectures, ultimately becoming a trusted friend and one of his three literary executors given the task of preparing his later works for publication. Anscombe's own work is dense and difficult; until recently it was not widely read beyond the circle of specialists. Yet her influence on twentieth century moral thought was enormous, and continues to be felt in the new millennium. Her 1958 article, "Modern Moral Philosophy," was like a healing salve applied to the thick hide of Anglo-American ethics. While it took time for her ideas to penetrate, they have had a lasting salutary effect. In those brief pages she pointed to the basic incoherence of contemporary debates over rules and consequences, suggesting that moral philosophy needed to consider anew the ideas integral to the classical conception of virtue. It needed to give an account of human action, human flourishing and the traits of character that make flourishing possible. The article became one of the principal catalysts in the revival of virtue ethics. Her own response to the challenge of renewal had begun the previous year with the publication of *Intention*. This brief collection of lectures reveals the inadequacy of many modern notions of will and is widely regarded as the founding text of contemporary theories of action.

Peter Geach (1916–) was prepared for a life in philosophy from an early age through the unique influence of his father. While Geach was still a teenager, his father had him reading the works of the Cambridge philosophers with whom he himself had studied: Bertrand Russell, G. E. Moore, John M. E. McTaggart, and the logical works of J. Neville Keynes. His father's interest in logic was to have a lasting influence on Geach, making him uniquely receptive to the works of Frege and Wittgenstein. Indeed, the consequences of logical errors for one's conception of the world and of oneself have been constant concerns in Geach's thought. Upon his conversion to Catholicism, Geach also began to read Thomas Aquinas, whom he studied directly without turning to the Thomistic manuals of philosophy. When interest in virtue ethics began to arise, it was often assumed that the rejection of an ethics of duty also implied a rejection of Christian moral perspectives such as the one espoused by Aquinas. A similar assumption was sometimes made concerning the rejection of internalist and abstractionist theories of knowledge: that by rejecting such theories, one was also rejecting the perspective of Aquinas. Geach was one of the first contemporary British philosophers explicitly to argue to the contrary. In *Mental Acts* (1957) Geach portrays Aquinas as an anti-abstractionist, while in *The Virtues* (1977) he presents Aquinas' moral theory as essentially virtue based, starting with the question of the purpose of human life.

Anthony Kenny (1931–) has traveled a religious path contrary to that of Anscombe and Geach. At the very time that the latter were reaching maturity in their Catholic faith, a faith lived with a feistiness equal to that expressed in Hilaire Belloc's *Path to Rome*, Kenny was losing his faith in a struggle he later described in his own *Path from Rome* (1986). As Roger Pouivet notes, however, it was precisely during this struggle that Kenny began to see the lasting value of Aquinas' moral psychology. His earlier studies – when still a diocesan priest studying at the Gregorian University in Rome – with the Jesuits Peter Hoenen and

Bernard Lonergan had already instilled in Kenny an admiration for Aquinas. Yet it was at Oxford through his contact with Anscombe and Geach as well as through his conversations with Herbert McCabe, O.P., that he became persuaded of Aquinas' lasting value for contemporary philosophy. Although Kenny regards Aquinas' ideas about God as outmoded, he maintains that Aquinas' understanding of cognition, practical reasoning, and human action remain deeply insightful. Kenny has defended this view and probed its implications both in works that study Aquinas directly and in his own attempts to develop an adequate account of knowledge and action.

Roger Pouivet draws on the work of these three authors to advance Wittgenstein's critique of the dominant modern conception of interiority. Wittgenstein does not deny that we have an interior life, but merely that this interiority is understandable in an absolutely private or non-communal way. At issue here is a picture of the self that comes close to portraying it as a little man inhabiting the body, a little agent who has unmediated knowledge of his passions, volitions and ideas as well as of himself as a thinking subject. In this picture, it is the inner life that is most certain; it is a world where these inner events are the first and direct objects of our consciousness. Secondarily, we know the world by means of them; or do we? Once this picture of the self is accepted, the question of its relationship to the outer world becomes paramount and problematic. Although the modern articulation of this view is from Descartes, its dualism has been a constant temptation in Western culture. Forms of it existed well before Descartes – having received its classical expression with Plato – while portions of it were embraced after Descartes by thinkers as diverse as Locke, Kant, and Husserl. Wittgenstein seeks to disenthrall us from this picture. Like the riddles of a Zen koan, the clipped and repetitive questioning of Wittgenstein's later work is meant to lead us to see how our inner life is the product of our initiation into the life and language of a community.

But to what extent do Wittgenstein's reflections encourage a return to a Thomistic or even an Aristotelian understanding of philosophy? Even if we grant that Wittgenstein's critique of Cartesian subjectivity is not a critique of Aquinas' understanding of the acting person, does Wittgenstein's analysis point toward the Thomistic view? Indeed, are not Wittgenstein's views on metaphysics and the limits of philosophy antithetical to Aquinas' understanding of what philosophy can discover about God, human immortality and the moral life? In responding to these questions we should recognize that Pouivet is not asserting that Aquinas and Wittgenstein share the same views about reason's ability to discover meaningful truths about God. As Anscombe notes in reference to natural theology, "Wittgenstein certainly worked and thought in a tradition for which this was impossible."[1] Nor is Pouivet claiming that Aquinas and Wittgenstein hold the same views on the moral life. Pouivet's claims are more modest. First, that Wittgenstein's critique of internalism renders Aquinas' perspective uniquely relevant for contemporary attempts to develop an externalist psychology of action. This is so because, as Anscombe, Geach, and Kenny have shown, Aquinas was an externalist: his understanding of human action and of practical reasoning was based not upon an a priori analysis of inner states, but upon an analysis of concrete human acts, an analysis that works backward toward the inner principles of action (intellect, will, and the emotions) and implies a recognition of the complex networks of human language and community on which these acts depend. Secondly, and this is the more controversial claim, Aquinas' conception of practical reasoning

---

1   Elizabeth Anscombe, "The Question of Linguistic Idealism," in *From Parmenides to Wittgenstein, the Collected Philosophical Papers I* (Oxford: Blackwell, 1981), 123.

and of human action is one direction toward which Wittgenstein's thought can legitimately be developed. This second claim minimally requires that Wittgenstein was neither a moral relativist nor a skeptic concerning at least some metaphysical principles. That he was neither a relativist nor an absolute metaphysical skeptic is the view advanced by Anscombe, Geach, and Kenny. For this philosophical triumvirate, Wittgenstein succeeded in developing a "realism without empiricism,"[2] that points to the fact that Aquinas' philosophy of mind and action "contains a structure which is fundamentally sounder than its modern rivals such as Cartesian dualism or scientistic materialism" and thus "is a structure on which future philosophers would do well to build."[3] This is Pouivet's argument; it is for the reader to decide whether he succeeds in advancing it convincingly. Whether or not one agrees with all of Pouivet's interpretations of the authors he studies, if his analysis succeeds in encouraging the reader to study Aquinas and Wittgenstein in light of the perspective on their works that Elizabeth Anscombe, Peter Geach, and Anthony Kenny have opened for us, then Pouivet will have obtained his goal.[4]

---

2   Ibid., 133.
3   Anthony Kenny, *A Life in Oxford* (London: John Murray, 1997), 146.
4   The relationship between Pouivet's Wittgensteinian Thomism and what has come to be known as Analytic Thomism remains an open question. For more on Analytic Thomism, see John Haldane, editor, *Mind, Metaphysics and Value in the Thomistic and Analytical Traditions* (Notre Dame: University of Notre Dame Press 2002). See also the special issues of the following three journals: *The Philosophical Quarterly* 43 (1993), *The Monist* 80 (1987) and *New Blackfriars* 80 (1999).

CHAPTER ONE
AN INTERNALIST INTERLUDE

From Wittgenstein to Saint Thomas

This study examines and attempts to justify Anthony Kenny's observation that, "In the eyes of many people, Wittgenstein's importance in the history of philosophy, and in particular of the philosophy of mind, lies especially in his criticism of the Cartesian framework within which philosophy and psychology had been conducted throughout the modern era, well beyond the critique of Kant. One side effect of Wittgenstein's liberation of philosophy from Cartesian prejudices is that it enables those who accept it to give a more sympathetic welcome to the writings of pre-Cartesian philosophers, and in particular medieval scholastics."[1] Even though Wittgenstein was assuredly not a commentator of Thomas Aquinas, by questioning the modern conception of mind and thought initiated by Descartes, Wittgenstein can establish for us a point of entry into the philosophy of Aquinas. The Kantian critique of rational psychology and of the Cartesian *cogito* did not eliminate the Cartesian perspective,[2] which in many ways

1   Anthony Kenny, *The Legacy of Wittgenstein* (Oxford: Blackwell, 1984), xi.
2   Immanuel Kant, "The paralogisms of pure reason," in *Critique of Pure Reason* (A 341/B 399–A 405/B 432) (Cambridge: Cambridge

is reaffirmed in the *Cartesian Meditations* of Husserl.[3] Strangely, it takes Wittgenstein, a philosopher of the twentieth century, to enable us to read with new eyes the work of Thomas Aquinas, a philosopher who precedes Wittgenstein by seven centuries and seemingly belongs to a very different intellectual horizon. How can we explain this strange occurrence?

To understand better how the reading of Wittgenstein can serve as a propaedeutic to the reading of Thomas Aquinas, we need first to understand three key terms: *externalism, internalism,* and *anti-individualism.* This abundance of "isms" is disconcerting, not only to linguistic purists, but also to those who value clarity in philosophical discourse. Leaving aside the issue of the linguistic wounds these "isms" inflict, we shall respond to the concern for clarity by defining the terms. These definitions will be indispensable, because the intention of this book is to show that Thomas and Wittgenstein are externalists and anti-individualists, and as such, stand in opposition to Descartes and to "modern philosophy" generally, which are internalist and epistemologically individualist.

Externalism affirms that at least certain factors justifying a person's beliefs are not accessible to him from an internal examination of his reasons for believing. Our beliefs are justified by the credibility of the processes that produce our

University Press, 1998), 411–58. The reason why the Kantian critique of the paralogisms of rational psychology does not have much impact is due principally to the character of transcendental philosophy itself and to the role it plays in the notion of an "internal sense." It would take us too far afield to treat this question here. For a study of this problem in Kant, see Peter F. Strawson, *The Bounds of Sense: An Essay on Kant's "Critique of Pure Reason"* (London: Methuen, 1966), 163–74.

3   Edmund Husserl, *Cartesian Meditations: an Introduction to Phenomenology* (The Hague: Martinus Nijhoff Publishers, 1960). On Husserl's ever-increasing idealism, see Roman Ingarden, *On the Motives Which Led Husserl to Transcendental Idealism,* translated by Arnor Hannibalssom (The Haag: Martinus Nijhoff, 1975).

beliefs, whether these are about the relationship between causes and their effects or between one belief and other relevant beliefs.[4] Alvin Plantinga has recently noted the contemporary reemergence of externalism in philosophy.[5] He explains that externalism goes back to Thomas Reid, and before him, all the way to Thomas Aquinas and to Aristotle. He even affirms that before Descartes, internalists (for whom the justification of our beliefs presupposes an internal examination of our reasons for believing) were rare. As possible pre-Cartesian internalists, he cites only St. Augustine and the skeptics from the later Platonic Academy. This suggests that the dominant philosophical tradition has been externalist, with internalism being a recent addition. Contemporary externalists would thus be returning to epistemological positions of more ancient origin in the history of philosophy. One could say that they are returning to the Aristotelian-Thomistic tradition after a Cartesian internalist interlude.

Unlike internalism, externalism is compatible with anti-individualism.[6] In other words, it is compatible with a theory that recognizes the fundamental role of the social environment (of belonging to a community) in defining the content of one's thoughts. The externalist thinks his beliefs justified because the process that engendered these beliefs is credible, while the internalist thinks his beliefs justified because he has examined the mental content of these beliefs to determine whether they fulfill certain necessary conditions for their epistemological justification.[7] If what

---

4 The externalist perspective has been clearly defined by Alvin Goldman, *Epistemology and Cognition* (Cambridge, Mass: Harvard University Press, 1986).

5 Alvin Plantinga, *Warrant: The Current Debate* (Oxford: Oxford University Press, 1993), v.

6 On anti-individualism, see Michel Seymour, *Pensée, langage et communauté: Une perspective anti-individualiste* (Paris: Vrin, 1994).

7 The best contemporary defense of a foundationalist and internalist position in the philosophy of knowledge is offered by Roderick M.

justifies our beliefs is not an internal examination of them, functioning on the Cartesian model as the *absolute* criterion of justification, then the examination of our reasons for believing can probably no longer be individual. Such an examination also involves what a community recognizes as the credible source of our beliefs. These beliefs are related to circumstances, to a certain state of affairs that causes them, and to a linguistic community to which we belong and in which we undergo an apprenticeship of decisive importance for our conceptual capacities, for our capacity for language. The externalism that Plantinga credits to St. Thomas[8] will be found to correspond – at least if one accepts the interpretation of Aquinas that I shall offer in this study – to the externalism and anti-individualism of Wittgenstein.

This post-Wittgensteinian reading of St. Thomas is present in the works of three British philosophers, Elizabeth Anscombe, Peter Geach, and Anthony Kenny. Kenny, who at the time was still a Catholic priest, studied philosophy in the English Athens that was Oxford at the end of the 1950s. Austin, Ryle, Hare, Strawson, Waismann, and Dummett taught there. Kenny states that from Peter Geach, "I learnt that an understanding of Wittgenstein and Frege could go along with a great admiration for Aquinas."[9] It was then (paradoxically at the very time he was distancing himself from the Vatican) that he was led to read seriously St. Thomas and Aristotle. In 1957 two books appeared that were fundamentally important for the post-Wittgensteinian reading of St. Thomas: *Mental Acts* by Peter Geach and *Intention* by Elizabeth Anscombe.[10] Later,

Chisholm, *Theory of Knowledge*, third edition (Englewood Cliffs, N.J.: Prentice-Hall, 1989).

8 The thesis that Thomas Aquinas is an externalist is also advanced by Eleonore Stump, "Aquinas on the Foundations of Knowledge," *Canadian Journal of Philosophy, Supplement*, vol. 17 (1991): 125–58.

9 Anthony Kenny, *A Path from Rome* (Oxford: Oxford University Press, 1985), 140.

10 Peter Geach, *Mental Acts* (London: Routledge, 1957; South Bend,

Anthony Kenny would also articulate clearly an interpretation of Thomas Aquinas and of Wittgenstein, especially in *Action, Emotion and Will*,[11] *The Anatomy of the Soul*,[12] *The Metaphysics of Mind*,[13] and *Aquinas on Mind*.[14] The works of these three philosophers could be described as constituting an original philosophical current: *Wittgensteinian Thomism*. This study presents their fundamental ideas, not only to facilitate one's reading of these three contemporary philosophers, but *above all* to encourage a joint reading of Wittgenstein and St. Thomas, where one explains the other.

Neo-Scholastic?

To reread St. Thomas in relation to contemporary questions, isn't this exactly what the neo-scholastics proposed at the end of the nineteenth century? A brief historical excursus will enable us to see that this is not the case. In his *Memoirs*, Ernest Renan contrasts "the barbarous and puerile scholasticism of the thirteenth century,"[15] with the education he received in the seminary at Issy. At Issy, he was taught "what we may term Cartesian scholasticism, that is to say the diluted brand of Cartesianism which was generally adopted for the instruction of the clergy in the eighteenth century, and had been codified in a work known as the *Philosophie de Lyon*."[16] Even though Victor Cousin labored to promote a fresh reading of medieval philosophy – of St. Thomas as well as of others – the spiritualism and positivism of France during the second half of the nineteenth century did not provide a favorable environ-

Ind.: St. Augustine's Press, 2001); Elizabeth (G. E. M.) Anscombe, *Intention* (Oxford: Blackwell, 1957).

11 Anthony Kenny, *Action, Emotion and Will* (London: Routledge, 1963).
12 Anthony Kenny, *The Anatomy of the Soul* (Oxford: Blackwell, 1973).
13 Anthony Kenny, *The Metaphysics of Mind* (Oxford: Oxford University Press, 1989).
14 Anthony Kenny, *Aquinas on Mind* (London: Routledge, 1993).
15 Ernest Renan, *The Memoirs of Ernest Renan (Souvenirs d'enfance et de jeunesse)*, translated by J. Lewis May (London: G. Bles, 1935), 161.
16 Ernest Renan, *Memoirs*, 161.

ment for such an endeavor. One had to wait until the pon-
tificate of Leo XIII, the encyclical *Aeterni Patris* of August 4,
1879, and the work of Maurice de Wulf at the *Institut
supérieur de philosophie* at Louvain, before St. Thomas could
find a place once again in philosophy, or even in theology.
In the work of historians of philosophy, the tradition of
Christian Aristotelianism emerged once again as distinct
from the Platonic Augustinian tradition.[17] This facet of the
scholastic renewal is well known in France in the works of
Etienne Gilson and Jacques Maritain.[18]

But the way of being Thomistic advanced by Geach,
Anscombe, and Kenny is entirely different. It is no longer a
question of criticizing modern thought in the name of a
Christian tradition ridiculed by Enlightenment rationalism,
as the neo-scholastics tended to do; nor is it even an
attempt to return medieval philosophy to its rightful place
in universities and other institutions of higher learning, as
the historians of medieval philosophy have often proposed. Instead, it is an effort to understand St. Thomas in
light of the possible reinterpretations of the *Summa theologiae* made available to us by Wittgenstein's *Philosophical
Investigations*. This approach is neither ideological nor historical, but philosophical, in the sense that, after
Wittgenstein we need the illuminating insights of the
Summa theologiae; we need the conceptual tools that are the
primary concepts of St. Thomas' philosophy. Geach or
Kenny will often on the same page go from Wittgenstein to
St. Thomas. There is no historical chasm between Thomas

---

17 For the history of this Neo-scholasticism, see Patrick J. Fitzpatrick,
"Neoscholasticism," in *The Cambridge History of Later Medieval
Philosophy*, edited by Norman Kretzmann, Anthony Kenny, Jan
Pinborg, and Eleonore Stump (Cambridge: Cambridge University
Press, 1982).

18 For an analysis of the different types of Thomism and their role in the
history of nineteenth- and twentieth-century philosophy, see
Alasdair MacIntyre, *Three Rival Versions of Moral Enquiry* (Notre
Dame, Ind.: University of Notre Dame Press, 1990), especially chapter three.

and Wittgenstein, or at least the chasm is not as large as the one between modern philosophers (Descartes or Kant) and Wittgenstein. This is what enables Thomas Aquinas, in the interpretation offered here, to come *after* Wittgenstein. Wittgenstein makes Aquinas more understandable and enables us to grasp the extent to which Aristotelian-Thomistic philosophy continues to be of great value. The goal of this current study is to demonstrate and to justify this interpretation of St. Thomas, an interpretation profoundly different from the one proposed by neo-scholasticism.

CHAPTER TWO
MENTAL ACTS

A Critique of Ryle

Can someone like Peter Geach, who wrote a book entitled *Mental Acts*,[1] be considered a Wittgensteinian? Did not
Wittgenstein constantly critique mentalism, which affirms
that psychological concepts signify and correspond to certain mental acts? As early as the *Blue Notebook*, Wittgenstein
shows that it is a mistake to describe thought as *mental
activity*. Surely it is just a metaphor to say that the mind
thinks? We are indeed tempted to locate thought somewhere, to describe it as the act of something in the mind.
Yet, if there are mental acts, shouldn't we be able to pose
the same questions about these acts that we pose concerning other acts, to question their nature, frequency, intensity,
and quality? To respond to such questions, however, causes us to fall into the myth of interiority, described at length
by Wittgenstein, who sought to liberate us from this myth's
troubling influence. The myth suggests to us that "a man's
thinking goes on within his consciousness in a seclusion in
comparison with which any physical seclusion is an exhi-
bition to public view."[2] Hence, "'I cannot know what is

1   Peter Geach, *Mental Acts*. (London: Routledge, 1957).
2   Ludwig Wittgenstein, *Philosophical Investigations*, translated by G. E.

going on in him' is above all a *picture*."[3] Is not the notion of a mental act also a picture? In other words, doesn't it also belong to the myth of interiority? Peter Geach offers a critique of a thesis advanced by Ryle in his book, *The Concept of Mind*,[4] a thesis that, in fact, was inspired by Wittgenstein. Nevertheless, Geach's critique of Ryle's thesis reveals how the notion of a mental act, which seems so un-Wittgensteinian, is actually at the heart of the Thomistic interpretation of Wittgenstein.

In Ryle's view, all statements containing psychological concepts to express mental events are actually reducible to hypothetical statements about observable behavior. Geach radically rejects this affirmation. We should note at the outset that Ryle is never *truly* able to maintain this behaviorist reductionism because he is never *really* able to dispense with psychological concepts. Yet, for Geach, the primary issue is Ryle's contention that the problem of counterfactuals is resolved. Let us suppose there are two individuals whose observable behavior is identical, but whose psychological preoccupations – in other words, their mental states – are different. We must then say that "the behaviour of one man *would have been* different from that of the other in hypothetical circumstances that never arose."[5] This explains their identical behavior in spite of their differing mental states. One must, therefore, have recourse to a conditional counterfactual.[6] In 1957 Geach could still say that the "the logic of counterfactual conditionals is a very ill-explored territory."[7] It would be difficult to hold this view today. Nevertheless, even though the problem of counter-

M. Anscombe, third edition (Oxford: Blackwell, 2001), II, xi, page 189.

3   Ludwig Wittgenstein, *Philosophical Investigations*, II, xi, page 190.
4   Gilbert Ryle, *The Concept of Mind* (London: Hutchinson, 1949).
5   Peter Geach, *Mental Acts*, 6.
6   A conditional phrase whose antecedent is manifestly false, for example: "if chickens had teeth, they would bite the ducks."
7   Peter Geach, *Mental Acts*, 6.

factuals has by now been explored, it has not yet been resolved.[8] Moreover, the way of exploring the problem – by means of logic, semantics, and a metaphysics of modalities[9] – merely relies on conceptual analysis without systematic development, which seems to have been Ryle's ideal of philosophy.[10] Thus, the Rylean interpretation of Wittgenstein is partly incorrect, because we cannot attribute to Wittgenstein the doubtful thesis that all mental acts are in the end nothing more than physical states.

According to Jacques Bouveresse, "it is clear that the eye of the mind would be completely blind if the agent did not have from the beginning a language and concepts to indicate and describe what he sees."[11] Hence, Wittgenstein affirms that our mental acts are not independent of language games, and consequently of our membership in a linguistic community and of our acquisition of language. This does not mean, however, that mental acts are illusory; nor does it imply that one can dispense with mental concepts. In critiquing Ryle, Donald Davidson says that "in general, the belief that one has a thought is enough to justify that belief. But, though this is true, and even obvious to most of us, the fact has, so far as I can see, no easy explanation."[12] Although it would be difficult to do this without imagining the mind as akin to a theater stage, a metaphor that Davidson explicitly rejects, this does not mean that therefore mental acts do not exist.

8   For an approach to this problem, see: David Sanford, *If P, then Q: Conditionals and the Foundations of Reasoning* (London, Routledge, 1989); see also, *Conditionals*, edited by Frank Jackson (Oxford: Oxford University Press, 1991).

9   Michael J. Loux, *The Possible and the Actual: Readings in the Metaphysics of Modality* (Ithaca, N.Y.: Cornell University Press, 1979).

10 Lucie Antoniol, *Lire Ryle aujourd'hui* (Bruxelles: De Boeck Université, 1993), 110.

11 Jacques Bouveresse, *Le mythe de l'intériorité* (Paris: Editions de Minuit, 1976), xi.

12 Donald Davidson, "Knowing One's Own Mind," in *Self-Knowledge*, edited by Qassim Cassam (Oxford: Oxford University Press, 1994), 43.

In the *Summa theologiae* (I 75.5),[13] St. Thomas affirms that the intellect can change. He notes, however, that when applied to the intellect "change" does not signify what it signifies when applied to matter, i.e., to a change occurring in something physical. Wittgenstein, for his part, emphasizes that "we may be led to an illegitimate assimilation of psychological to physical reports."[14] Wittgenstein does not reject the private *reference* of these psychological expressions – for no one else can experience my toothache for me – but the notion that the *meaning* of these psychological expressions can be grasped interiorly in relation to a wholly interior event.[15] What Wittgenstein contests here is the notion that we can portray the interior observation of oneself as analogous to the way we observe external things – and that we can apply this same analogy to interiority and intimacy. In such cases, since the word "observation" is not employed in the same way, it does not have the same meaning, just as the word "change" does not mean the same thing when applied to the intellect as when applied to matter.[16]

Wittgenstein does not consider it illusory to believe that our mental acts have a content (to see the train arrive, to await a letter, to think that one is in love, etc.); nor does he regard it as illusory to hold that we express this content in sentences ("we see the train arrive;" "I am awaiting a

13 From here on, the *Summa theologiae* is abbreviated as *ST*. For an explanation of the method of referring to the *ST*, see the Selected Bibliography at the end of this volume.
14 Peter Geach, *Mental Acts*, 2.
15 The principal texts concerning this point are those found in §243 and following of Wittgenstein's *Philosophical Investigations*, part I.
16 David M. Armstrong, operating from a materialist theory of mind, advances exactly the opposite thesis: "In sense-perception we become aware of current happenings in the physical world. A perception is therefore a mental event having as its (intentional) object situations in the physical world. In introspection, on the contrary, we become aware of current happenings in our own mind" (David M. Armstrong, "Introspection," in *Self-Knowledge*, edited by Quassim Cassam [Oxford: Oxford University Press, 1994] 109).

letter;" "I think that I am in love."). At least certain mental acts, therefore, are acts of judgment that we express verbally by means of indirect discourse (*oratio obliqua*).[17] Acts of judgment both presuppose concepts and, in a certain sense, express them. Hence, Geach can affirm that, "I thus accept the psychology of the old logic-books, to the extent of recognizing the possession of concepts as presupposed to acts of judgment, and regarding a judgment as the exercise of a number of concepts."[18] From Wittgenstein we retain here the view that concepts cannot be expressed at the level of simple apprehension. In other words, they cannot be expressed by themselves independently of a particular language game. Yet, for Geach, this in no way invalidates the psychology advanced by Thomas Aquinas. The concept is the *species*[19] produced by the intellect. This species is intentional to the extent that it is mental and not physical. It corresponds to one part of the mental word. One might object that this is the opposite of Wittgenstein's view, and that we are on the verge of falling into the private-language fallacy. This, however, is not the case, for as Geach explains, "to say that a man has a certain concept is to say that he can perform, because he sometimes *does* perform, mental exercises of a specifiable sort."[20] The concept is a disposition to think this or that. It is a mental potentiality expressed in language and in other symbolic activities.

In commenting on St. Thomas (ST I 85.5), Anthony Kenny explains that "'Intelligible species' are the acquired mental dispositions which are expressed, manifested, in intellectual activity: the concepts which are employed in the *use of words*, the beliefs which are expressed by the *use of sentences*. My grasp of the meaning of the English word

17 Peter Geach, *Mental Acts*, 7–10.
18 Peter Geach, *Mental Acts*, 14.
19 This term signifies (here) the form as thought.
20 Peter Geach, *Mental Acts*, 15. In an illuminating passage, Geach states that, "acquiring a concept is a process of becoming able *to do something*" (Ibid., 18).

'rain' is one kind of species; my belief that red night skies precede fine days is another kind of species."[21] The thesis attributed to Aquinas by Kenny is the same one advanced by Geach from a Wittgensteinian perspective, but freed from Ryle's behaviorism. Geach is thus led to offer a critical remark concerning the pretensions of certain psychologists. They employ the same terms – "conceptual competence" – to describe a human being's understanding of a triangle and a brute animal's understanding of a triangle. Geach does not explicitly cite Thomas, but it seems clear that he draws on the teaching of the *Summa theologiae* (I 8.4): if humans and animals are virtually identical on the level of sense impressions, the difference between them resides in the distinction between the natural estimative faculty in animals, which is an instinct, and the human cogitative faculty, which is properly intellectual and consists in the expression of concepts. Concerning conceptual expression, Thomas Aquinas and Wittgenstein speak with one voice. To say that an animal recognizes a triangle is to have a strange idea of what the concept of a triangle is!

Abstractionism

Geach rejects what he calls "the characteristic abstractionist view of psychological concepts," according to which "they are abstractively derived from *inner* experience."[22] He notes that according to this perspective, "we are supposed to possess a quasi-sense that is related to psychical occurrences in much the same way as our senses are to physical occurrences."[23] In Geach's approach, when it is a question of logical, mathematical, or relational concepts or of concepts such as color, the rejection of the abstractionist perspective corresponds to the Wittgensteinian critique of

21 Anthony Kenny, *Aquinas on Mind* (London: Routledge, 1993), 46. Emphasis added.
22 Peter Geach, *Mental Acts*, 21.
23 Ibid.

ostensive definition.[24] When it is a question of psychological concepts, the rejection of the abstractionist perspective corresponds to the Wittgensteinian critique of a private language, which critique proceeds as follows. A language presupposes rules. Moreover, respect for rules presupposes that assent or dissent from the rules be public, for nothing can guarantee the proper use of a private rule. In other words, it would be impossible during the private use of a rule to distinguish between following the rule and believing that one is following the rule. Consequently, the very idea of a private language is not only psychologically dubious, it is *logically* absurd. The private-language critique highlights the mythic character of the view that meaning is an interior event by means of which a symbol becomes a signifier. The private language critique is more fundamental than the critique of ostensive definition because it encompasses it. One supposedly focuses attention on an aspect of an object *stripped* of all its other characteristics. For example, one focuses on its being large or small. One then claims that the concepts *large* or *small* are acquired by abstraction from large or small things, things that have in common being large or small. The act of attention at the source of this abstraction is presented as an interior event. One next affirms that the meaning of concepts, whatever they may be, depends on this internal effort of attention directed toward their meaning. There would thus exist an interior ceremony of discriminating and designating an aspect of an object by the *attention* we focus on an event occurring within us. Even if Geach does not explicitly say it this way, abstractionism is also a target of the Wittgensteinian critique of private language. The ostensive definition by means of which the abstract aspect of an object is designated always presupposes this interior atten-

---

24 Ostensive definition signifies definition by direct designation, such as pointing at an object with one's finger. In other words, it is definition by drawing *particular attention* to the very thing designated.

tion, this effort that everyone must make to determine within themselves the meaning of the concepts they use. The very thing Wittgenstein shows to be absurd is presupposed by all the philosophers who depend upon the internalist justification of beliefs proposed by Descartes in his *Second Meditation*.

How can we break with internalism? On this point, chapter eleven of *Mental Acts* is significant. It is entitled, "Making Concepts Is Not a Finding of Recurrent Features." Geach mixes here Fregean, Thomist, and Wittgensteinian considerations that harmonize well.

Frege. We should consider the concept as a (mathematical) function and not as an object existing independently of us (Platonism), whatever may be the nature of the object in question.[25]

St. Thomas. Reflections on question thirteen of the *Summa theologiae*: can we form affirmative propositions about God? St. Thomas responds that we can. One could counter that since God exists without composition and since an intellect when it affirms knows its object through composition and division of concepts, one cannot construct an affirmative proposition concerning God. Thomas responds to this argument as follows:

> The assertion that every intellect that understands something otherwise than it is, is false, can be taken in two ways, according to whether we take the adverb "otherwise" to modify the verb "to understand" in reference to the intellect or in reference to the act of understanding. If in reference to the intellect, then the affirmation is true and means the following: every intellect that understands a thing to be different than it is, is false. But this affirmation does not apply in the current case, because our intellect in forming a propo-

25 See Gottlob Frege, "Function and Concept," and "On Concept and Object," in *Translations from the Philosophical Writings of Gottlob Frege*, edited by Peter Geach and Max Black (Oxford: Blackwell, 1952), 21–55. See also below, chapter four.

sition about God does not affirm him to be composite, but simple. If, instead, the proposition is applied in reference to the act of understanding, then it is false, because the way the intellect exists in the act of understanding differs from the way the thing exists in itself.[26]

Geach follows Thomas in affirming that "when our understanding understands things that are simple, it may understand them in its own complex fashion without understanding them *to be* complex."[27] The mind *makes* concepts; it does not find them ready-made by the mere power of a so-called abstractive method. Yet, this does not prevent us from applying these concepts to reality, to the knowledge of something, when we apply them correctly. Geach adds that "we must resist the perennial philosophical temptation to think that if a thought is to be true of reality, then it must copy it feature by feature, like a map."[28] At this point, we pass from Thomas Aquinas to Wittgenstein, who questions in his later philosophy his own thesis from the *Tractatus* concerning precisely this erroneous view of language as an image of reality.[29]

26 *ST* I 13.12 ad 3: "*haec propositio, intellectus intelligens rem aliter quam sit, est falsus, est duplex, ex eo quod hoc adverbium aliter potest determinare hoc verbum intelligit ex parte intellecti, vel ex parte intelligentis. si ex parte intellecti, sic propositio vera est, et est sensus, quicumque intellectus intelligit rem esse aliter quam sit, falsus est. sed hoc non habet locum in proposito, quia intellectus noster, formans propositionem de deo, non dicit eum esse compositum, sed simplicem. si vero ex parte intelligentis, sic propositio falsa est. alius est enim modus intellectus in intelligendo, quam rei in essendo.*"

27 Peter Geach, *Mental Acts*, 40.

28 Ibid., 41. One could consider that *in fact* a map does not copy reality feature by feature – to the extent that this idea makes sense, because does reality have features as such? – but the one who makes the map chooses representative characteristics. See Roger Pouivet, *Esthétique and logique* (Liege: Mardaga, 1996), chapter two, particularly, page 75.

29 See *Tractatus logico-philosophicus*, translated by D. F. Pears and B. F. McGuinness, introduced by Bertrand Russell (London: Routledge, 1974), §§2.1 to 2.225.

Wittgenstein. Geach explains that "linguistic capacities, for an abstractionist, are necessarily an external, adventitious aspect of the possession of concepts."[30] All of the later philosophy of Wittgenstein tirelessly denounces this abstractionist thesis. St. Thomas offers a similar correction. "Words, therefore, do not signify the intelligible species [contrary to what Plato claimed], but that by which the intellect itself forms judgments about exterior things [as Aristotle holds]."[31]

By juxtaposing Frege, Thomas Aquinas, and Wittgenstein, this brief historical tour shows that the three philosophers share a common view of the concept as a *function* by means of which objects are characterized. The function is a *means*, not an object. It is an intellectual tool revealed in linguistic activity. It is not an intentional entity.[32]

It could nonetheless seem strange to appeal to the authority of St. Thomas in rejecting abstractionism, a thesis sometimes attributed to him. We need, therefore, to explain the role played in Thomas' thought by the notion of an *agent intellect* (a conceptual capacity). In other words, we need to consider that for which, in Aquinas' view, a concept functions. At this point, the analogy between light and the agent intellect could prove useful: light is to vision what the agent intellect is to understanding (to conceptual comprehension). For Thomas:

> There are two opinions concerning the role of light. Some say that light is necessary for sight in order to make colors visible in act. In this way, the agent intel-

30 Peter Geach, *Mental Acts*, 44.
31 *ST* I 85.2 ad 3: "*non ergo voces significant ipsas species intelligibiles; sed ea quae intellectus sibi format ad iudicandum de rebus exterioribus.*
32 An intentional entity would be a *meaning* to which the concept would refer, a meaning independent of language and even of intellectual activity. Moreover, Frege gives a place for the notion of *Sinn*, but he distinguishes it *firmly* from the notion of concept. See Anthony Kenny, *Frege* (London: Penguin, 1995).

lect is necessary for understanding in order to play the same role as light in the act of seeing. Others, however, affirm that light is necessary for sight not in order to make colors actually visible, but in order to render the medium of sight actually luminous, as Averroes states in the second book of his commentary on the *De Anima*. According to this interpretation, the analogy that Aristotle employs to compare the agent intellect to light must be interpreted as follows: just as light is necessary for sight, so too is the agent intellect necessary for understanding, but not in the same way.[33]

Commenting on this passage, Kenny explains that "one can think of the agent intellect as like the lantern a miner carries in his helmet, casting the light of intelligibility upon the objects a human being encounters in his progress through the mysterious world."[34] Things in the physical world are only potentially thinkable or intelligible. This is why an animal, even if it has the same senses as we, or even senses more acute than ours, cannot know things *specifically*: that is to say, it cannot know them by means of that which makes them be what they are. The agent intellect, as a capacity for abstract thought, for producing universal intentional species, makes knowledge possible.[35] It is by linking the intentional species to sensible experience that we know individuals (particular things), and that we can form singular propositions. There are no humans nor humanity without an agent intellect that thinks in terms of the humanity of this or that being; the agent intellect,

33 *ST* I 79.3 ad 2: *"circa effectum luminis est duplex opinio. quidam enim dicunt quod lumen requiritur ad visum, ut faciat colores actu visibiles. et secundum hoc, similiter requiritur, et propter idem, intellectus agens ad intelligendum, propter quod lumen ad videndum. secundum alios vero, lumen requiritur ad videndum, non propter colores, ut fiant actu visibiles; sed ut medium fiat actu lucidum, ut commentator dicit in ii de anima. et secundum hoc, similitudo qua aristoteles assimilat intellectum agentem lumini, attenditur quantum ad hoc, quod sicut hoc est necessarium ad videndum, ita illud ad intelligendum; sed non propter idem."*
34 Anthony Kenny, *Aquinas on Mind*, 47.
35 *ST* I 85.1.

however, is not thinking about a mere idea having nothing more than mental existence. It is this that makes the concept (or intelligible species) equivalent in many respects to the Fregean notion of the concept as a mathematical function. The agent intellect is a properly human capacity to know the real *through* intentional or intelligible species.

This perspective is very far from an abstractionist model. According to Geach,[36] the difference between the two perspectives is clearly illustrated in a text from the *Summa theologiae* (I 85.2 ad 3) where St. Thomas explains that our use of concepts should not be compared to the act of seeing something, but to the act of forming a visual image of something that we do not now actually see, or even of something that we have never seen. Thus, not only is the formation of concepts not abstractionist; neither is their use. Geach notes also that abstractionism is incompatible with the theory of substance developed by Thomas Aquinas. Admittedly, one can hold that Thomas exaggerated the ease and certitude of our knowledge of the *quod quid est* (the essence) of a thing, that he wasn't sufficiently receptive to the arguments of the skeptics. Yet, this is a separate issue.[37] From a Thomistic perspective, it is difficult to see how by mere abstraction one could pass from sensate knowledge to knowledge of an intelligible species. Abstractionism could, no doubt, have a Lockean or a Humean epistemology, but certainly not an Aristotelian or Thomistic epistemology.

The Conceptual Disposition

What the Thomistic and Wittgensteinian conceptions of mind truly share in common is the notion that the human intellect is the totality of our dispositions to acquire and

36 Peter Geach, *Mental Acts*, 130.
37 Nor can we discuss here the question concerning whether or not Wittgenstein accords any real weight to the arguments of the skeptics. This is an important and highly controverted issue in contemporary interpretations of Wittgenstein.

exercise knowledge – to *know that* as well as to *know how*. To view the conceptual capacity in terms of acquisition and exercise is to view it as a disposition. Every exercise is the secondary actualization of a disposition, which is itself the primary actualization of a capacity.[38] Thus, the human person has a rational capacity actualized in conceptual dispositions that are exercised when we say a sentence such as "the cat is on the carpet," as well as when we do something, such as open the refrigerator door to see if there is any milk. Wittgenstein notes that "The grammar of the word 'knows' is evidently closely related to that of 'can,' 'is able to.' But also closely related to that of 'understands.' ('Mastery' of a technique.)"[39] Kenny clarifies that, "The mastery of a particular concept – the understanding, for example, of the word 'inflation' – is a particular disposition of the intellect."[40]

It is surprising to see the extent to which Wittgenstein's efforts to deconstruct a model of knowledge that viewed cognition in terms of mental processes accompanying what we say or do – efforts he pursued from the 1930s to practically the end of his life[41] – led him to embrace something St. Thomas holds very naturally, the notion of conceptual dispositions. All those strange contortions of Wittgenstein's later philosophy (those series of remarks that lead us from one problem to the next, only to lead us back to the previ-

---

38 Anthony Kenny states that, "A disposition . . . is halfway between a capacity and an action, between pure potentiality and full actuality" (*The Metaphysics of Mind* [Oxford: Oxford University Press, 1984], 84).
39 Ludwig Wittgenstein, *Philosophical Investigations*, I §150.
40 Anthony Kenny, *The Metaphysics of Mind*, 84. What is the difference between a disposition and a habit? "If one has a disposition to do X then it is easier to do X than if one has not: examples are being generous and speaking French. If one has a habit of doing X then it is harder not to do X than if one has not: examples are smoking and 'I say' before each sentence" (ibid., 85).
41 For example, see the texts written during 1947 and 1948, published in *Remarks on the Philosophy of Psychology*, edited by Georg H. von Wright and Heikki Nyman, translated by C. G. Luckhardt and M. A. E. Aue (Oxford: Blackwell, 1980), vol. II, §722.

ous one, but now viewed from a different perspective) all act to untie the knot of internalist philosophy. This does not mean, however, a return to the old, pre-Cartesian scholasticism. Rather, it leads us to read St. Thomas, and his medieval contemporaries, in a new way. What Wittgenstein describes as tempting perspectives (for example, that something is joined to the words we use, "which otherwise would run idle"[42]) typically correspond to an internalist philosophical thesis often held by the intellectual progeny of Descartes. Such perspectives, however, were not yet current in the age of Aquinas. St. Thomas views the soul in terms of "powers." These powers become manifest in the very actions we attribute to them and which they exercise. They are not something residing *behind* this activity. Thus, according to Kenny, the intellect is "the capacity for understanding and thought."[43] Thought is a capacity made manifest in our speech and in our actions; it is absolutely not a process that accompanies them. Such a process would do little more than reify the disposition, as when one was led, in a caricature of Aristotelianism, to speak of the dormitive power of opium.[44] Opium certainly causes one to sleep, but the disposition is not the cause of the sleeping. Sleep merely reveals what opium *does*. The disposition is defined by its act. The concept is nothing other than the act itself of understanding; understanding is not something that accompanies the concept or its verbal expression.

For St. Thomas the intellect is both "possible" and "agent."[45] Its possibility consists in its capacity to receive thoughts;[46] its activity in its capacity to produce objects of thought:[47] "It is necessary, therefore, to posit the existence

---

42 Ludwig Wittgenstein, *Philosophical Investigations*, §507.
43 Anthony Kenny, *Aquinas on Mind*, 41.
44 Anthony Kenny, *The Metaphysics of Mind*, 72–73.
45 See the summarizing text from *ST* I 54.4.
46 *ST* I 79.2.
47 "Object of thought" should not be understood as an intentional entity that could itself exist independently of the understanding one has

of a power in the intellect that can render objects actually intelligible by abstracting the species from their material conditions."[48] The distinctiveness St. Thomas' position among his contemporaries was his assertion that the agent intellect was not a supernatural agent acting upon humans in external and mysterious ways.[49] The agent intellect is a capacity proper to everyone who thinks. It is the *capacity to learn*. Echoing this position unawares, Wittgenstein states: "It could also be said that a man thinks when he *learns* in a particular way."[50] What way is this? It is the way of learning we attribute to humans and not to animals or angels. Indeed, concerning angels we not only can doubt whether they need to learn, we can doubt whether they can learn.[51]

There is, therefore, a close relationship, for Thomas as well as for Wittgenstein, between a perspective that views thought as both a capacity (possibility or potentiality) and its exercise (activity), and one's perspective on learning.

of the object existing independently of the mind. As Quine says, "the points of condensation in the primordial conceptual scheme are things glimpsed, not glimpses" (*Word and Object* [Cambridge, Mass: MIT Press, 1960], 1). For a discussion of this question, from a perspective close to that of Geach and Kenny, see Vincent Descombes, *Objects of All Sorts: A Philosophical Grammar*, translated by Lorna Scott-Fox and Jeremy Harding (Baltimore: Johns Hopkins University Press, 1986), 49–61; and *Les institutions du sens* (Paris: Éditions de Minuit, 1996), 9–94. See also below, chapter four.

48 *ST* I 79.3: "*oportebat igitur ponere aliquam virtutem ex parte intellectus, quae faceret intelligibilia in actu, per abstractionem specierum a conditionibus materialibus.*"

49 See St. Thomas' *Against the Averroists: On There Being Only One Intellect*, translated by Ralph McInerny (West Lafayette, Ind.: Purdue University Press, 1993).

50 Ludwig Wittgenstein, *Zettel*, edited by Elizabeth (G. E. M.) Anscombe and Georg H. von Wright; with an English translation by G. E. M. Anscombe (Chicago: University of Chicago Press, 1967), §105.

51 *ST* I 54.4 If humans learn, it is because they must actualize an intellectual capacity that is only possibly active, and hence the role of the agent intellect. Consequently, "in angels, knowledge is not generated, it exists in them naturally" (*ST* I 54.4 ad 1).

Neither Thomas nor Wittgenstein regards thought as an interior process accompanying certain activities such as speech or reasoning. Wittgenstein explains that, "To begin by teaching someone 'that looks red' makes no sense. For he must say that spontaneously once he has learnt what 'red' means, i.e., has learnt the technique of using the word."[52] To learn what red is, is to learn how to use the word. To learn how to use this word (to learn to react in a certain way) presupposes a capacity in which a certain disposition can take root and a certain activity can take place. This disposition, the disposition to use "red," is not a process parallel to and distinct from the use itself. Yet, contrary to what Ryle suggests, at least in certain excessively behaviorist passages of *The Concept of Mind*, neither does this mean that we can reductively regard such activity as a behavior, in principle, describable in non-psychological terms. Wittgenstein affirms that, "What thinking is might be described by describing the difference between someone feeble-minded and a normal child who is beginning to think. If one wanted to indicate the activity which the normal person learns and which the feeble-minded cannot learn, one couldn't derive it from their behaviour."[53] This activity, which is not parallel to the use that is made of "red" or of some other concept, but consists in the use itself, and yet is not reducible to a merely behaviorist description of the action, this is what Thomas calls *understanding*. It is the proper act of the agent intellect, producing the concepts by means of which it classifies the phantasms (sense images) that the possible intellect stores, the possible intellect being understood here as the recipient of information received causally from sensible things.[54]

52 Ludwig Wittgenstein, *Zettel*, §418.
53 Ludwig Wittgenstein, *Remarks on the Philosophy of Psychology*, vol. II, §11.
54 St. Thomas states that "the sense images (phantasms) are not only illuminated by the agent intellect, the agent intellect by its power also abstracts the intelligible species from them" (*ST* I 85. 1 ad 4).

Human Nature

One can legitimately question the role given here to capacities and dispositions in the development of knowledge. It seems to depend on an exceedingly obscure notion of potentiality. Indeed, isn't the ancient doctrine of natural species hidden in this critique of modern philosophy, a critique that marks a return to the Aristotelian conception of intellect? Doesn't this doctrine affirm that each thing has a proper nature that defines its future and defines its capacities in relation to the potentialities of its species? Although this may be a legitimate interpretation of Aquinas' philosophy, which is clearly amenable to such a view, aren't we going too far to attribute such a thesis to Wittgenstein? This is not the place to discuss natural species and its possible contemporary relevance for the philosophy of mind. Nevertheless, following the lead of Israel Scheffler, we should at least support a view that "interprets the *potential* possession of a characteristic at a given time as implying its *manifest lack* at that time and asserting in addition the capacity to acquire the characteristic in question at some time in the future."[55] Our conceptual activity presupposes a natural capacity, the capacity proper to humans as a species endowed with a certain nature: human nature. This capacity should be understood as a possibility, in the sense that, "to say it is *possible* that such-and-such is to say that it is not *necessary* that *not* such-and-such."[56] The intellect is possible in exactly this way: it is *potential*. It is an agent when it actualizes this potentiality in intellective dispositions. The possible is well defined by our humanity, which is itself defined by our capacity to think (and to will). It is not easy to see how the fact of being human could be mere-

---

Concerning the notion of a phantasm, see the appendix at the end of this study.

55 Israel Scheffler, *In Praise of the Cognitive Emotions* (London: Routledge, 1991), 26.

56 Ibid. Emphasis in the original.

ly a matter of chance or choice and not of nature.[57] The intellect as potentiality is the capacity to acquire multiple and varied dispositions, to *know that* and to *know how*, and the dispositions that actualize these capacities are the result of learning.

Wittgenstein remarks with astonishment, "What a strange phenomenon that a child can actually learn human language! That a child who knows nothing can start out and learn by a sure path this enormously complicated technique. This thought occurred to me when on a certain occasion I became conscious of how a child starts *with nothing* and one day uses negations, just as we do."[58] We are tempted to say to Wittgenstein, "does it really start with nothing?" A potentiality is certainly nothing that guarantees any particular outcome outside of the circumstances in which it is actualized, as, for example, when a child employs negation as we do. Yet, a potentiality does ensure that nothing inhibits a child from one day employing negation as we do. (It is not *necessary* that the child not achieve this activity.)[59] We know this from the very moment of his birth, even though he is at that time still unable to do so. The applicability of the predicate "capable of employing negation as we do," assures, in a certain sense, that one belongs to our species, to one and the same nature. To think of the mind in terms of potentiality is to insist on the notions of capacity, disposition, and the activity that reveals the disposition, which is itself the actualization of a capacity.

---

57 See the insightful critique of Sartre by Etienne Gilson in "Réponses à quelques questions," (appendice 2) in *L'être et l'essence* second edition (Paris: J. Vrin, 1962), 357–64.
58 Ludwig Wittgenstein, *Remarks on the Philosophy of Psychology*, vol. II, §128.
59 Even in the case of the mentally handicapped, it is not necessary that they not achieve it.

CHAPTER THREE
AGAINST DESCARTES

The Internal Sense

The conception of mental acts proposed in the final section of the previous chapter brings to the fore a specific philosophical tradition. It is a tradition from within which the Wittgensteinian critique of the myth of interiority provides a point of entry into St. Thomas' philosophy of mind. This chapter will assert that this tradition is resolutely anti-Cartesian.

The critique of the view that we possess an inner sense focuses on the meaning of psychological concepts, and on the way we learn to use them correctly. As Geach notes,[1] the proponents of the internal sense sometimes compare it to sight (introspection) and sometimes to impression.

> People suppose that I can give meaning to such words as "seeing," "hearing," "thinking," "hoping," etc., only by observing in my own case sample occurrences of what these words refer to; failing the relevant experiences, or failing attention to them when I have them, I must either lack a concept altogether or possess it in a very imperfect form, comparable to a colour-blind man's concept of colours.[2]

1   Peter Geach, *Mental Acts*, 107.
2   Ibid., 108.

This is what seems to render the existence of an internal sense not only credible, but even indispensable for the use of psychological concepts. Yet, the notion of an internal sense is neither credible nor necessary. That it is not credible becomes clear when we ask, for example, whether one can be blind to an emotion in the same way one can be blind to the distinction between green and red. Could one have a congenital defect in the internal sense to such a degree that, although one remained perfectly intelligent, one was unable to identify correctly one's emotions? How far can we take the analogy between the internal and external senses? We might be tempted to respond that the internal sense differs from external senses such as sight, because the internal sense is *infallible*. I cannot be wrong concerning my interior world. Here we have a thesis of Cartesian origin.

For Descartes, one cannot be mistaken about the passions of the soul: "they are so close and so internal to our soul that it cannot possibly feel them unless they are truly as it feels them to be."[3] Our passions are pure mental events and do not rest on any conjecture concerning the cause of these events. This is why they are infallible. One could certainly respond that even if we don't ground the passions in a physical cause, the immediate cause of a passion is a movement from the pineal gland, initiated by the animal humors, while the cause of the gland's movement is some object acting on our senses. Nevertheless, a passion is not felt in the pineal gland, "unless the soul truly has this passion within it."[4] Error or ignorance of this cause, there-

---

3 René Descartes, *The Passions of the Soul*, §26 (AT 11: 348) in *The Philosophical Writings of Descartes*, vol. 1, translated by J. Cottingham, R. Stoothoff, and D. Murdock (Cambridge: Cambridge University Press, 1985), 338. (In citations of Descartes' works, the numbers in parentheses refer to the standard twelve-volume French edition of his works edited by Charles Adam and Paul Tannery [hence AT]: *Oeuvres de Descartes* [Paris: Vrin, 1964–1976]. The first number refers to the volume, while the second refers to the page. –*Trans.*)

fore, in no way alters each person's certitude concerning his own passions.

Let us now compare this view with the perspective of Thomas Aquinas. He understands by "passion" everything connected with affectivity, which he distinguishes from sense perception and the intellect.[5] The soul does not have passions except as united to a body; passions are reverberations in the soul of changes in the body, which cause the body to pass from one state to another. This is why the passions are something we undergo. For St. Thomas "the soul is united to the body in two ways: in one way as the form, which gives being to the body and vivifies it. In a second way, as a mover, for it is through the body that the soul exercises its operations."[6] Thus, the soul can suffer indirectly (*par accidens*) when the body is wounded. This would be an example of bodily passion. Yet, in the case of anger, or fear, or similar emotions,

> the passion begins in the soul, as the mover of the body, and ends in the body. Consequently, this type of passion is called an animal passion,[7] . . . for it arises as a consequence of a perception and desire of the soul, from which there follows a change in the body, as occurs when a movable object receives the action of a mover, according to the different ways that the movable object is receptive to following the motion of the mover."[8]

4   René Descartes, *The Passions of the Soul*, §26 (AT 11: 349) in *The Philosophical Writings of Descartes*, v. 1, p. 338.
5   *ST* I-II 22.1.
6   *De Veritate* 26.2: "*unitur [anima] autem corpori dupliciter: uno modo ut forma, in quantum dat esse corpori, vivificans ipsum; alio modo ut motor, in quantum per corpus suas operationes exercet.*"
7   Aquinas is alluding here to the fact that the word *animal* is derived from the Latin word "soul" (*anima*). – *Trans.*
8   *De Veritate* 26.2: "*incipiat [passio] ab anima, in quantum est corporis motor, et terminetur in corpus; et haec dicitur passio animalis; . . . nam huiusmodi per apprehensionem et appetitum animae peraguntur, ad quae sequitur corporis transmutatio. sicut transmutatio mobilis sequitur ex operatione motoris secundum omnem modum quo mobile disponitur ad obediendum motioni motoris.*"

Thus, strictly speaking, emotion has nothing to do with an interior perception by means of an internal sense, which would make me aware of my anger, my sadness, my fear, or my other emotions. Man is intellect and will, intellectual appetite and sense appetite. His faculty of desire depends above all on the idea he has of objects, and through this idea, upon the objects themselves. In contrast to the rational appetite, sense appetite depends on the soul because the soul is linked to the body. Since, therefore, the emotions are the result of the union of body and soul, the emotions become incomprehensible once one affirms that they are indifferent to the existence of the body. For Descartes, the passions are felt in the soul. For Thomas, the passions are not directed toward objects of an internal sense, but toward *objects in the world*. The passions are ways of making these objects present. They are not interior states indifferent to the objects themselves, apprehended interiorly, in other words, independently of their objective causes.

To call into question the Cartesian thesis concerning the passions of the soul is to undermine the foundations of idealism. Idealism affirms the existence of a knowledge that is entirely independent of the fact that we have a body. Idealism is concerned only with thought itself, with pure mental representations, ideas, intentional experiences – with almost anything but concrete sensible things. This idealist thesis can take a strong form, as in Descartes' *Second Meditation*. The strong form is especially present in Husserl's analyses, which are predicated upon the ability, by means of a phenomenological reduction, to suspend the thesis of a world (the existence of things outside of myself) and by means of which the transcendental self is supposedly revealed as subjectivity existing of itself and for itself.[9]

9 Edmund Husserl, *Erste Philosophie (1923/24)*, vol. 2 (Husserliana vol. 8), edited by Rudolf Boehm (The Hague: Martinus Nijhoff Publishers, 1959), 82–131. Transcendental phenomenology, at least in its transcendentalist form, is exactly what Wittgenstein rejects. It affirms that phenomenological consciousness finds, without going outside itself (one is inevitably led to employ this strange *metaphor*),

The idealist thesis can also take a weak form. There is, for example, the Humean theory of idea in which, according to Geach, one simply confuses the mental image of a thing with the exercise of a concept of it in judgment.[10] There is also the transcendental idealism of Kant, which is always linked, in spite of everything, to an empirical realism. Here, we shall primarily challenge the strong form of idealism. Yet, by contesting the Cartesian thesis, we are not jumping from the frying pan only to fall into the fire. In rejecting philosophical reflection about psychological concepts, we are not forced to embrace the neurosciences in their effort to eliminate *pop psychology* in favor of the physical sciences.[11] Man is a being composed of a soul (or mind if one prefers) and a body, where the first is the form of the second. It is this composite that we should understand, and not merely one aspect of it (soul or body) to the detriment of the other.

We are humans, body and soul: this is the Thomistic teaching. This teaching encounters significant difficulty when it attempts to understand the torments that can afflict incorporeal spirits, such as the demons. Should we attribute suffering to them, as well as emotions, even though they do not have bodies, being only pure spirits?

the object at which it aims. Thus, one speaks of objects, but as limited to the immanence of consciousness. The word "object," therefore, has an extraordinary meaning, even though it more or less continues to be employed in the ordinary way. For example, it is affirmed that we can describe the "object" in question, although all the conditions that ordinarily make description possible have simply disappeared. Does christening these descriptions as part of a "transcendental egology" (*Erste Philosophie*, 129) resolve anything? (See below, chapter four.)

10 Peter Geach, *Mental Acts*, 108.
11 This project is clearly expressed, for example, by Stephen P. Stich in *From Folk Psychology to Cognitive Science* (Cambridge, Mass: MIT Press, 1983). For a discussion of this project, see Pascal Engel, *Philosophie et psychologie*, collection folio 283 (Paris: Gallimard, 1996), especially chapter five.

> Fear, pain, joy, and similar things, if they are consid-
> ered as passions, cannot exist in the demons; they
> belong properly to the sense appetite, which is the
> power of a corporeal organ. But, as naming a simple
> act of the will, they can exist in the demons. Since
> pain, as a simple act of the will, is nothing other than
> the will's revulsion against what is or is not, the
> demons must experience pain. This is clearly the case
> because the demons wish many things were that are
> not, and wish many things were not that are. For, since
> they are envious, they wish the saved to be damned.[12]

Thus, the "passions" of the demons, from the fact that they
are incorporeal, are not, as in humans, what the soul suffers
in relation to the body, but stem from the perversity of their
wills. Passion is in the "soul" itself of the angel and in the
soul alone. Internalism, therefore, applies to humans a psychology that properly belongs to angels . . . and to demons.

The thesis of the internal sense is not in any way necessary to explain our use of psychological concepts; in fact, it
is an obstacle to this explanation. Take, for example, the
term "to see." The meaning of this word does not come
from an internal experience that we can describe, analyze,
and show how, as an internal experience, it gives meaning
to the term "to see." Knowing that we see would thus come
from turning our attention to an interior phenomenon, the
vision of something. Knowing that I see would presuppose
interior observation of what happens to me when I see
something, whether or not I actually see something;
whether or not there actually is something for me to see.
Once this step has been taken – once all reference to the

12 *ST* I 64.3: "*timor, dolor, gaudium, et huiusmodi, secundum quod sunt
passiones, in daemonibus esse non possunt, sic enim sunt propriae
appetitus sensitivi, qui est virtus in organo corporali. sed secundum quod
nominant simplices actus voluntatis, sic possunt esse in daemonibus. et
necesse est dicere quod in eis sit dolor. quia dolor, secundum quod significat
simplicem actum voluntatis, nihil est aliud quam renisus voluntatis ad id
quod est vel non est. patet autem quod daemones multa vellent non esse
quae sunt, et esse quae non sunt, vellent enim, cum sint invidi, damnari eos
qui salvantur.*"

effective use of the term "to see" is removed, and with it the notion that to see signifies seeing real characteristics of existing things and that those who see these things act in certain ways – a theory of the internal sense becomes indispensable to explaining the meaning of the term *to see*. Yet, as Geach explains, from a Thomistic as well as a Wittgensteinian perspective,

> What shows a man to have the concept seeing is not merely that he sees, but that he can take an intelligent part in our everyday use of the word "seeing." Our concept of sight has its life only in connexion with a whole set of other concepts, some of them relating to the physical characteristics of visible objects, others relating to the behaviour of people who see things.[13]

We certainly would not say that a person sees a chair before him, when in fact there is a table. Nor would we say that he knows what "to see" means if he were to say that someone sees, when the someone in question claims to see a chair, where in fact there is only a table, and we are assured that he knows the meaning of "table." To know that one sees and what it means to see – to see something as humans see them – presupposes something entirely different from an internal sense. It presupposes something that has much more to do with the intelligent use of the term "to see."

Such a use of the term "to see" always presupposes public verification, since it is governed by rules guiding what belongs under a given concept – and the notion of a private rule is by definition a contradiction in terms (*contradictio in adjecto*), as Jacques Bouveresse affirms.[14] The vocabulary that enables me to identify my own seeing of something, my own thoughts, beliefs, and feelings, depends in great part on a linguistic community; it even depends on exterior objects and events. This is what leads Putnam to insist

13 Peter Geach, *Mental Acts*, 112.
14 Jacques Bouveresse, *Le mythe de l'intériorité*, 429.

that meanings "just ain't in the head."[15] What a word means depends on the way we have learned it. Consequently, the perceptions, thoughts, beliefs, intentions, and hopes that we express in words should, because of exterior objects and events, be recognizable as belonging to those who have them. As Davidson says, commenting on Putnam, "If meanings ain't in the head, then neither, it would seem, are beliefs and desires and the rest."[16] How can we isolate a purely subjective sphere in which thoughts, beliefs, and desires can be identified independently of all non-subjective, exterior factors, and which would enable me to identify my perception, thought, belief, desire, as being the perception or thought of this, the belief in that, or the desire for this or that thing?[17]

We are entitled, therefore, to abandon the notion that the use of psychological concepts rests upon the operation of an internal sense, thanks to which the meaning of psychological terms is referred to thoughts, the contents of consciousness, interior experiences or to some sort of mental event.

15 Hilary Putnam, "The Meaning of 'Meaning,'" in *Mind, Language and Reality, Philosophical Papers II* (Cambridge: Cambridge University Press, 1975), 227.
16 Donald Davidson, "Knowing One's Own Mind," 46.
17 This problem has also been thoroughly treated by Tyler Burge, "Individualism and the Mental," *Midwestern Studies in Philosophy* 4 (1979): 73–121, reprinted in *Basic Topics in the Philosophy of Language*, edited by Robert M. Harnish (Englewood Cliffs, N.J.: Prentice-Hall, 1994), 393–446; "Individualism and Self-Knowledge," *Journal of Philosophy* 85 (1988): 649–63, reprinted in *Self-Knowledge*, edited by Qassim Cassam (Oxford: Oxford University Press, 1994), 65–79. It has been treated from the same perspective as Burge by Michel Seymour, who seeks to show that "public linguistic conventions are a necessary condition for the existence of intentional mental states" (*Pensée, langage et communauté*, 20). This position is most properly called *anti-individualism*. See also Tyler Burge, "Cartesian Errors and the Objectivity of Perception," in *Subject, Thought, and Context*, edited by Philip Pettit and John McDowell (Oxford: Clarendon, 1986), 117–36.

The Error of the Cogito

The critique of the notion of an internal sense prepares us to question an essential Cartesian concept: the concept of the thinking "I." Wittgenstein in a passage from the *Big Typescript* says:

> In the theories and battles of philosophy we find words whose meanings (*Bedeutungen*) are well-known to us from everyday life used in an ultra-physical sense. . . . (Philosophers are often like little children, who first scribble random lines on a piece of paper with their pencils, and then ask an adult "what is that?" – Here's how this happened: now and then the adult had drawn something for the child and said: "That's a man," "That's a house," etc. And then the child draws lines too, and asks: now what's that?).[18]

This is what happens with the *cogito*. In ordinary daily life, I say "I" in order to attract attention to myself. Everyone does this and for the same reason. To attract attention to myself is to attract attention to R.P. Now, in a solitary soliloquy I can say, "I am stupid this morning," or some such thing, as one might say to oneself while looking in the mirror or rereading one's own work. In this case, I am clearly not trying to draw attention to myself, to signal to myself that it is truly I who speak. Geach explains this clearly:

> what is going to count as an allowable answer to the question "What is this 'I'?' or "Who then am I?" These questions might have a good clear sense in certain circumstances – e.g. if Descartes had lost his memory and wanted to know who he was ("Whom am I?"

---

18 Ludwig Wittgenstein, "Philosophy" (Sections 86–93 [pp. 405–35] of the so-called "Big Typescript" [Catalog Number 213]) in *Philosophical Occasions 1912–1951*, edited by James Klagge and Alfred Nordmann (Cambridge: Hackett, 1993), 193. "Philosophy" is one of the four chapters of the "Big Typescript" not edited and published by Rush Rhees as *Philosophical Grammar*. For more on the curious fate of this chapter of the "Big Typescript," see Anthony Kenny, "From the Big Typescript to the Philosophical Grammar," in *Essays on Wittgenstein in Honor of G. H. von Wright, Acta Philosophica Fennica* 28 (1976): 41–53. *–Trans.*

"You are René Descartes."), or if he knew that some-
body had said "I'm in a muddle" but not that it was
himself ("Who is this 'I' – who said he was in a muddle?" "You did."). The states of mind that would give
the questions sense are queer and uncommon, but
they do occur. But no such rare circumstance was
involved in Descartes's actual meditation; in the actual conditions, it is simply that the questions "Who am
I?" "Who is this 'I'?" are deprived of any ordinary use
and no new use has yet been specified.[19]

In other words, what Descartes proposes is to use the term
"I," but to give it a completely different meaning from the
one it normally has when it indicates that this or that person is speaking, yet continuing to act *as if* the problem really were to know what "I" signifies when it is employed in
a meditative soliloquy and not in a conversation with others. It is clear who is speaking when I say "I." It is me, R.P.
Who is speaking when I say "I," but am not speaking to
anyone else? This is what Descartes would have us ask. Yet,
if I can in some way talk to myself about myself, this is not
because I have grasped within myself who I am, a thinking
substance – my egologic life, as it will soon be described –
but because I know how to use "I" when I say "I" in order
to attract attention to myself (R.P.). The extraordinary use is
"parasitic," as Geach says,[20] upon this ordinary, psychological, but not Cartesian, or transcendental or phenomenological, use of "I." This questionable Cartesian usage pro-
motes an entire philosophy of consciousness around what
is perhaps simply an ill-considered question concerning an
inappropriate use of the word "I." This is why Geach
describes the *cogito* as "a blind alley."[21] It is, however, the
alley taken by a good number of thinkers in modern philosophy.[22]

19 Peter Geach, *Mental Acts*, 118–19.
20 Peter Geach, *Mental Acts*, 120.
21 Peter Geach, *Mental Acts*, 121. (A "dead end" in American English.
    –*Trans.*)
22 One could respond that this is to forget Marx, Freud, Heidegger,

Many commentators have entered the Cartesian framework. The real question for them is how to understand the
structure of this ego, the ego of the *ego cogito*, which isn't
this or that person, but the "egoeity" of someone's ego, that
which makes him a subject. Such formulations seem to
underpin an approach whose principal challenge seems to
be to explain how any of it makes any sense. Those who,
from early infancy to high school, have become accustomed by their philosophical wet nurses to see in Cartesian
thought an unprecedented philosophical advance (the discovery of subjectivity as auto-foundational), will interpret
Geach's critique as the sign of an irreparable metaphysical
blindness, if not of a naiveté as disappointing as it is
British. Geach disengages from the Cartesian perspective
as quickly as possible, without going into the details. It is
the Cartesian use of the word "I" that is distorted.
Descartes supposedly discovered a self disencumbered, at
long last, of its psychological rags, as also the transcendental self and the phenomenological self will claim to be; in
the final analysis, however, these selves aren't the selves of
anyone. This "discovery" is essentially an act of linguistic
violence. Geach offers his perspective as follows:

> If we believed in "inner-sense," we might say . . . : "In
> order that I should say 'this pain waxes and wanes
> regularly,' it is not enough that I should think of *pain
> regularly waxing and waning* and the pain be there; the
> pain must fall before my mind's eye, my 'inner sense,'
> as the cat and the liver fall before my bodily eye." But
> this is just mythology. All I need in order to judge
> about the pain is that my thinking of *pain-waxing-and-*

Foucault, Derrida, among others. Yet, (1) the anti-subjectivism of
these philosophers has not hindered the development, especially in
France, of a transcendental phenomenology (Merleau-Ponty or even
Ricoeur); (2) the rejection of the *cogito* that these philosophers have
proposed or suggested is clearly not inspired by St. Thomas, and for
fairly clear reasons, it is completely incompatible with Thomism,
whether the latter be viewed as a religious or a purely philosophical
teaching (see below, chapter six).

waning should stand in the *conversio-ad-phantasmata*[23] relation (whatever that may be) to the pain itself – not to some sensation of "inner sense," whereby I am cognizant of the pain. Similarly, suppose I momentarily think I have lost my keys, ferret for them in my pocket, and then report: "How odd! A pang of panic came *after* my fingers had actually touched the keys!" The bits of my sense-experience to which there is now *conversio* are the feeling of the keys and the feeling of panic; there is no "inner" sensation in which I see or feel the panic and discriminate its panicky quality – there is only the feeling of panic itself.[24]

In other words, we can indeed explain the proper nature of psychological concepts, of my impressions, my emotions, my thoughts, and so forth, without presupposing the existence of a substantial reality, the self, having these impressions, emotions, thoughts – i.e., without portraying them as *properties* of the self. We are essentially rejecting here the private character of our thoughts, emotions, feelings, etc. We are rejecting the notion that there is an interior world, which would then require us, to the extent that this is still possible, to understand how this inner world can be connected to the external world of bodies, both my own and those of other minds. Our thoughts are not interior events of which we could become conscious by paying attention to the life of the self, whether this be through introspection or through a Husserlian bracketing of the world. Although Descartes never affirmed that we have an interior eye, he unfortunately inaugurated in philosophy the modern thesis according to which, as Bouveresse describes it, "the mind has some sort of sense or quasi-sense that enables it to maintain with its contents, operations and products the same type of relationship that it maintains with the external world by means of the senses."[25]

23 In other words, directed toward sensible things.
24 Peter Geach, *Mental Acts*, 123.
25 Jacques Bouveresse, *Le mythe de l'intériorité*, 523. As Bouveresse notes (ibid., 524), Descartes cannot be classified as an abstractionist (see the

Privatism

Privatism maintains that the psychological concepts proper to humans acquire their meaning in relation to an interior event internal to the mind. Wittgenstein rejects this possibility. A person knows what to think means, not because he is able to engage in the unique operation of grasping what he is, a thinking thing, but because he is human. He does certain things that those who think do: he speaks, he solves different types of problems, mostly practical ones; he smiles at what is funny; he becomes annoyed, and so forth. All these things happen among human beings who have no difficulty recognizing each other as humans, except in exceptional cases or when the person has been blinded by ideology. On the street, people do not greet machines, but their friends and neighbors. With respect to sensations, if one wishes to follow St. Thomas, one cannot say with Descartes that even if animals show signs of pain comparable to the ones we observe in humans, they are merely refined natural automatons. Even though they are sensate instead of rational creatures, animals have a soul. On the other hand, as Kenny states, "The [human] mind itself can be defined as the capacity for behaviour of the complicated and symbolic kinds which constitute the linguistic, social, moral, economic, scientific, cultural, and other characteristic activities of human beings in society."[26]

What is rejected here, therefore, is dualism, the thesis that there are two worlds, the physical and the psychological, where the latter is private and inaccessible to public

preceding section). Yet, in this instance, it matters little whether one posits an inductive genesis of ideas or regards them as innate. The problem of the meaning of mental concepts remains the same. As Bouveresse states, "the issue above all is to know what we 'have in the mind,' as Descartes would say, while we have the idea of pain. In other words, the issue is whether the concept of pain, to the extent that it has been acquired, corresponds or not to an immediate, private experience, in the sense criticized by Wittgenstein" (ibid., 526).

26 Anthony Kenny, *The Metaphysics of Mind*, 7.

observation. Descartes, the British Empiricists up to Bertrand Russell, as well as the Phenomenologists, all describe the mind in terms of consciousness and not in terms of the capacity to use different types of symbolic systems. In this way, Descartes clearly broke with the venerable tradition of conceiving the human mind not in terms of an interior world but in terms of intelligence and rationality. Aristotle, Thomas, and Descartes all hold that humans alone possess language, but this observation does not imply for the first two what it implies for the latter. For Descartes, it reveals that only humans are minds. It thus reinforces his dualism. If animals don't speak it is because they don't have a soul.[27] In contrast, for Aristotle and the Christian Aristotelians, the intellect in humans is to a certain extent the capacity to make intelligent use of words and phrases. The capacity for language is certainly proper to humans, but it has nothing to do with the distinction between body and soul. It pertains instead to the essential difference that having an intellect makes. St. Thomas states:

> The word of our intellect . . . is that in which the operation of our intellect terminates, which is the intellect itself, and is called a conception of the intellect; it can be a conception expressed either by a simple expression, as occurs when the intellect forms the quiddities of things, or by a complex expression, as occurs when the intellect composes and divides.[28]

The theological significance of the term "word" – the question of the difference between the divine Word and the human word – is an issue that lies beyond the scope of this current project. For us, what is important here is the "very

27 René Descartes, *Discourse on the Method*, part 5 (AT 6:55–60) in *The Philosophical Writings of Descartes*, v. 1, p. 139–41.
28 De Veritate 4.2: "*verbum intellectus nostri, . . . est id ad quod operatio intellectus nostri terminatur, quod est ipsum intellectum, quod dicitur conceptio intellectus; sive sit conceptio significabilis per vocem incomplexam, ut accidit quando intellectus format quidditates rerum; sive per vocem complexam, quod accidit quando intellectus componit et dividit.*"

close relationship between thought and words, between the operation of the intellect and the use of language."[29] With Thomas Aquinas this relationship appears clearly in the overlap between the operations of the intellect and the characteristics of language. The species correspond to the understanding of words, our beliefs to enunciated compositions and divisions. Thomas does not hold that the intellect's sole activity is linguistic, but he does affirm that the intellect's activity is linked to our linguistic capacity, and understood in the use we make of this capacity.

After Wittgenstein we better understand what this way of viewing the mind's activity entails. For Wittgenstein,

> While we sometimes call it "thinking" to accompany a sentence by a mental process, that accompaniment is not what we mean by a "thought." – Say a sentence and think it; say it with understanding. – And now do not say it, and just do what you accompanied it with when you said it with understanding! – (Sing this tune with expression. And now don't sing it, but repeat its expression! – And here one actually might repeat something. For example, motions of the body, slower and faster breathing, and so on.)[30]

It is not an illusion to say that thought is something other than language, or even that language expresses thought. Yet, one runs the risk of acting as if thought were a process that gives language its meaning, a process that is in principle detachable from language and to which we could have independent access. One would then have fallen into the Cartesian theory of language as an indication of thought.[31]

Thomas and Wittgenstein say something entirely different. Language does not reveal the existence of a private interior process to which the subject alone has access. That we speak demonstrates the opposite: our intelligence

29 Anthony Kenny, *Aquinas on Mind* (London: Routledge, 1993), 49.
30 Ludwig Wittgenstein, *Philosophical Investigations*, I §332.
31 René Descartes, *Discourse on the Method*, part 5 (AT 6:56-58) in *The Philosophical Writings of Descartes*, v. 1, p. 139–41.

consists in the use of language, and thus in the mastery of a linguistic common good. The linguistic capacity is not an indication of interiority, but an indication that the intellect is related to one's social and linguistic membership. Wittgenstein asks, "But couldn't we imagine God's suddenly giving a parrot understanding, and its now saying things to itself? – But here it is an important fact that I imagined a deity in order to imagine this."[32] Prescinding from the question of the deity, one could ask what would happen if a parrot were to say, "I think, therefore I am"? What is the "I" at work here? One would sense that it lacks *something* in the parrot, what Wittgenstein also calls, "a dream of our language."[33] One would certainly be tempted to locate this something in a consciousness that has direct access to the very thing that makes the *cogito* said by Descartes different from one said by a parrot, and not to appeal to a certain way of using the language under certain conditions, within a particular *language game*. Yet, upon careful reflection, what distinguishes the two is that I do not attribute to the parrot what I attribute to humans, a rational capacity exhibited in everything he says and does. Even though the parrot speaks, I do not attribute interiority to him. Speech is not a sign of interiority; I only attribute interiority to those who speak (which Descartes certainly holds), and therefore to those who are proficient in something *common* and *public* (which Descartes clearly does not hold). It is not because each of us has an interior life that we can learn to speak, but because we have learned to speak that each of us can have an interior life.

Thomas does not insist specifically on the relationship between thought and language, even though he conceives of intellectual operations according to the linguistic modes of definition, affirmation, division, and so forth. He is writing *before* the advent of the very idea of consciousness as a

32 Ludwig Wittgenstein, *Philosophical Investigations*, I §346.
33 Ludwig Wittgenstein, *Philosophical Investigations*, I §358.

place where meanings reside. Wittgenstein, however, is writing *after*. Thus, he must confront an internalist thesis that has become almost a sort of philosophical reflex. In this sense, by his labors, Wittgenstein facilitates our understanding of St. Thomas and of the thesis that the rational activity of the human person is not a form of internal representation but is the exercise of the concept.

CHAPTER FOUR
INTENTIONALITY

Esse Naturale and Esse Intentionale
(Mode of Natural Existence and Mode of Intentional Existence)

Phenomenology is commonly presented as the resurgence of the medieval question of intentionality. Credit is often given to Brentano, but above all to Husserl, who supposedly knew how to withdraw the question of intentionality from *psychologism*. Yet, was there no other medieval heritage of intentionality than phenomenology? Wasn't there a medieval heritage of intentionality present in Wittgenstein's thought, even if he himself never perceived this heritage?

As Kenny remarks,[1] the problem of intentionality is explicitly addressed by Wittgenstein in section five of the first part of the texts published under the title *Philosophical Grammar*. This passage seems particularly clear: "'How does thought manage to represent?' – the answer might be 'Don't you really know? You certainly see it when you think.' For nothing is concealed."[2] Wittgenstein also states:

1   Anthony Kenny, *The Legacy of Wittgenstein*, 61.
2   Ludwig Wittgenstein, *Philosophical Grammar*, edited by Rush Rhees, translated by Anthony Kenny (Berkeley: University of California Press, 1974), part 1, n. 63, p. 104.

"'I thought Napoleon was crowned in the year 1805.' – What has your thought got to do with Napoleon? – What connection is there between your thought and Napoleon?"[3] What makes a thought of an X a thought *of an* X? This, according to Kenny, is the problem of intentionality. Wittgenstein for his part affirms that: "A strange process, this meaning!"[4] and also: "meaning something is like going up to someone."[5]

Thomas Aquinas responds to the problem of intentionality by developing his doctrine of the immaterial, intentional existence of forms in the mind. The theory of mental acts we advanced in chapter two, before undertaking our critique of Cartesian privatism in chapter three, revealed the inadequacy of the thesis that there is a mental entity, such as an idea, that represents the thing for which it is the idea. Instead of this thesis, we advanced one that portrays the mental act as the exercise of a concept, in other words, as an act of the intellect. This act refers to something in the act of thinking it. The mind does not form a mental representation of it, as an idea corresponding, in the best of cases, to what the thing is in itself. The thesis advanced by St. Thomas is that in the act of knowing there is a *formal* (but not a *material*) identity between the extra-mental object and the faculty of understanding, i.e., the intellect. In the example of a horse, "The form exists, individualized and enmattered, in the real horse; it exists, immaterial and universal, in my mind."[6] This is the difference between *esse naturale* and *esse intentionale*.

What makes a sensation or thought of an X, to be a thought *of an* X, is an event of the same form (or nature) as what makes an X the thing that it is. This form now exists intentionally and not naturally, which is how it occurs in its

3   Ludwig Wittgenstein, *Philosophical Grammar*, part 1, n. 62, p. 103.
4   Ludwig Wittgenstein, *Philosophical Grammar*, part 1, n. 62, p 103.
5   Ludwig Wittgenstein, *Philosophical Investigations*, I §457.
6   Anthony Kenny, *The Legacy of Wittgenstein*, 62.

real existence. As Geach clarifies, "there may be cases in which X-ness [the form of X] has only *esse intentionale* in my mind without there being any X-ness in the physical world – but this does not mean that my mind stands in relation to a non-existent reality."[7] One arrives at the thesis of the identity between the knower and the known in knowledge, a thesis that is inadmissible and simply scandalous to modern philosophy. For Thomas, in knowledge thought *is* the form itself; it is an intentional but nonmaterial occurrence of the form, in other words, of the nature of the thing thought. It is not a relation with this form; it is not an intentional aiming at the form, distinct from it; it is the form itself under a certain cognitive mode. How are we to understand this thesis, which appears so strange to anyone formed by Kantianism?

The Corruption of Logic and Its Noetic Consequences

If the Thomistic doctrine of forms is disconcerting to the modern mind, this is primarily due to a problem of *logic*: to the continued influence of the two-term theory of predication. According to Geach,[8] Aristotle at first held, following Plato, that *onoma* and *rhema* (name and predicable) were mutually exclusive. Apart from the fact that negation never applies to the name,[9] the name's logical role is simple: the name designates an entity and, therefore, it does not have parts that signify on their own. This is the theory of the

---

7   Elizabeth Anscombe and Peter Geach, *Three Philosophers* (Oxford: Blackwell, 1973), 95–96. Thomas, therefore, does not adopt a theory that leaves room for nonexistent objects (as does Meinong) or for *sense-data* (as does Russell).

8   See Peter Geach, "History of the Corruptions of Logic," in *Logic Matters* (Oxford: Blackwell, 1972), 44–61.

9   For a fuller discussion of this problem, see Jacques Bouveresse, "La théorie de la proposition atomique et l'asymétrie du sujet et du prédicat: deux dogmes de la logique contemporaine?" in *Mérites et limites des méthodes logiques en philosophie* edited by Jules Vuillemin (Paris: Vrin, 1986), 79–119.

syntactic simplicity of the subject. After holding this beautiful doctrine in the *De Interpretatione* (*On Interpretation*), Aristotle subsequently abandons it in his later works. As Geach explains,

> Whereas the *rhema* was regarded as essentially predicative, "always a sign of what is said of something else," it is impossible on the new doctrine for any term to be essentially predicative; on the contrary, any term that occurs in a proposition predicatively may be made into the subject-term of another predication.[10]

This is the Aristotelian theory of interchangeability. It marks a shift from an authentic subject-predicate theory to the *two-term theory*. It leads logicians to question the syntactic simplicity of the subject, because a predicate that does not have this simplicity can itself become the subject of predication. For Geach, "Aristotle's going over to the two-term theory was a disaster, comparable only to the Fall of Adam."[11] Only a (proper or common) name should be treated as a logical subject, because it alone can designate an individual.

Theorists will subsequently slip from a two-term theory into a two-name theory, in which *to designate* is identified with *to be predicable*.[12] From then on, "is" will have to be considered a *copula*. Since a simple series of names would be unintelligible, something is needed to link two names together.[13] The copula must be a copula of identity. We then arrive at the most perverse and degraded form of this logical doctrine: the two-class theory. In "Socrates is a philoso-

---

10 Peter Geach, "History of the Corruptions of Logic," in *Logic Matters*, 47.

11 Ibid.

12 See Peter Geach, "Logic in Metaphysics and Theology" in *Logic Matters*, 289–27. See also the (critical) discussion of Geach by Cyril Michon, "Asymétries: Thomas d'Aquin et Guillaume d'Occam précurseurs de Frege," *Les Études philosophiques* 3 (1996): 307–20.

13 Peter Geach, "History of the Corruptions of Logic," in *Logic Matters*, 53.

pher," "the term 'philosopher' *denotes* the class of all philosophers, but *refers* to just a part of the class."[14] With respect to "Socrates," this term takes the place of a class that only has one member.[15] On the other hand, with Frege and Russell, we come once again to recognize the categorical difference between name and predicable.[16] A reader of "On Concept and Object"[17] and of "On Denoting,"[18] often does not perceive that their authors, Frege and Russell (who are sometimes described as the gravediggers of Aristotelian logic), propose an *Aristotelian* logical teaching, one found in the *Categories* and in *On Interpretation*. They distinguish firmly between the name designating an individual entity and a predicate viewed as a sign of what is said of a thing. Today, one would refer to an argument x, and to a function F, and one would say that a proposition has the form $F(x)$.[19]

14 Ibid.
15 Leibniz advances essentially the same thesis when he suggested we treat singular propositions (i.e., referring to one individual entity) like universal or particular propositions. "Socrates is mortal," would thus have as its contrary negation, "no Socrates is mortal." See Gottfried Leibniz, "A Paper on 'Some Logical Difficulties,'" in *Logical Papers*, edited, translated and introduced by G. H. R. Parkinson (Oxford: Clarendon, 1966), 115–21 (*Die Philosophischen Schriften*, edited by Karl. I. Gerhardt [Berlin: Weidmann, 1890], vol. 7, pp. 211–17). We leave aside here the thorny problem of an empty class.
16 Peter Geach, "History of the Corruptions of Logic," in *Logic Matters*, 59. See also, Jacques Bouveresse, "La théorie de la proposition atomique et l'asymétrie du sujet et du prédicat," 80–81.
17 Gottlob Frege, "On Concept and Object," in *Translations from the Philosophical Writings of Gottlob Frege*, edited by Peter Geach and Max Black (Oxford: Blackwell, 1952), 42–55.
18 Bertrand Russell, "On Denoting," in Bertrand Russell, *Logic and Knowledge: Essays, 1901–1950*, edited by Robert Charles Marsh (London: George Allen and Unwin, Ltd, 1956), 39–56.
19 See Gottlob Frege, "On sense and Reference," in *Translations from the Philosophical Writings of Gottlob Frege*, 56–78, for the reemergence of this thesis in 1891, although clearly under a new form. We should also recall that the distinction had been discussed, in the context of early analytic philosophy, by Frank P. Ramsey (*Philosophical Papers*, edited by D. H. Mellor [Cambridge, Cambridge University Press,

In what way does this history of logic understood as a fall and redemption concern the problem of intentionality? It does so by means of the notion of form. We have seen that there is a formal identity between the extra-mental object and the concept thanks to which the object is thought and recognized as what it is. Geach further affirms that, "For Aquinas, the real distinction between a form and the self-subsistent individual (*suppositum*) whose form it is comes out in the logical distinction between subject and predicate (Ia q. 13 art. 12; q. 85 art. 5 ad 3 um)."[20] St. Thomas is not guilty of the sin of the two-name theory.[21] The predicate does not designate anything. It is not a some-thing: it is true or false *of* certain things.[22] Hence, "the wis-dom of Socrates" is not the wisdom that Socrates possess-es, since "wisdom" does not designate an individual entity. Wisdom becomes an individual entity only from within a platonic perspective, something which St. Thomas firmly refuses to embrace.[23] As Geach explains, "What refers to a form is 'the wisdom of . . .', not the whole phrase 'the wis-dom of Socrates'; 'the wisdom of . . .' needs to be complet-ed with a name of something that has the form, just as the predicate '. . . is wise', which also stands for this form,

1990], 12). See also, Frederic T. Sommers, *The Logic of Natural Language* (Oxford: Oxford University Press, 1982), especially chapter two, for a (very critical) discussion of Geach (and Frege).

20 Peter Geach, *God and the Soul* (London: Routledge, 1969; South Bend, Ind.: St. Augustine's Press, 2001), 43.

21 Peter Geach, "Logic in Metaphysics and Theology," in *Logic Matters*, 300. The distaste that Geach displays for the two-name theory is no doubt due to the heretical consequences for theology which, in his view, the theory contains: "the two-name theory leads inevitably to grave distortions of Catholic dogma, and is therefore not a relatively harmless speculative error" (ibid., 292).

22 *ST* I 45.4: "Since, therefore, accidents, forms and such like, do not subsist, being realities that coexist instead of exist, they should be described as co-created instead of created, for it is proper to created things to be subsistents (*sicut igitur accidentia et formae, et huiusmodi, quae non subsistunt, magis sunt coexistentia quam entia; ita magis debent dici concreata quam creata. proprie vero creata sunt subsistentia.*)."

23 *ST* I 79.3.

needs to be completed by a subject."[24] Thus, a destructive logical theory, the two-name theory, will distort foundational ontological, noetic, and logical insights of Aquinas' thought. Just as the name takes the vacant place in the predicative phrase ("Socrates"*completes* the expression "the wisdom of . . ."), the individual entity (Socrates) is thought about to the extent that it individualizes a form (Wisdom). In "The wisdom of Socrates," the "of" does not introduce a relation of "inherence in" or of "belonging to."[25] It would be better to consider "the wisdom of Socrates" as the *instantiation* of a form in Socrates; in other words, Socrates is an occurrence of the form that is wisdom. Thus, when we know that Socrates is wise, what we know is not his "inherence in" or "belonging to" the collection of wise things, but an individualized form, the form of the wise Socrates, even though we know this in terms of the concept of wisdom. Instead of being something in which Socrates inheres, what is known is *in esse intentionale* what exists *in esse naturale* in Socrates. In other words, what is known is an individual thing as instantiating the properties that it has. This individual object is known through the production of a (universal) concept that the object instantiates.

There is no intermediary entity,[26] no intentional object constructed by the thinking subject and by means of which the real object is considered, since what is known is an individual thing *to the extent that* it instantiates certain forms apprehended by the mental act that constitutes the concept. As St. Thomas states, what is directly known is the universal by means of the intelligible species, "while what are indirectly known are the singulars, from which come the phantasms."[27] The statement that "nothing can be understood except immaterially,"[28] implies, therefore, that there

24 Peter Geach, *God and the Soul*, 48.
25 Ibid., 49.
26 See Etienne Gilson, *The Christian Philosophy of St. Thomas Aquinas* (New York: Random House, 1956), p. 476, n. 17.
27 *ST* I 86.1: *"indirecte autem singularia, quorum sunt phantasmata."*
28 *ST* I 86.1 ad 3: *"nihil intelligitur nisi immaterialiter."*

is no direct knowledge of individual things. Instead, individual (material) things are known only indirectly, by means of a universal (and thus also by means of a certain mental act that produces the concept) to the extent that the individual instantiates the universal (humanity, wisdom, etc.). Clearly, if one accepts the view that predicates are interchangeable with subjects, this theory of intentionality, which regards concepts as universals *in esse intentionale* by means of which we know individual things, becomes unintelligible. One would thus have to posit some means by which thought could be linked to humanity and felineness, just as it is linked to Socrates or to this small cat. One would thus distort the character of the intentional mental act, failing to see that it is always linked to particular things, even though it only knows these particular things by means of universal concepts. If the universals always serve as predicates, this is precisely because they are never – except reflexively in a secondary act of knowing – the subject of knowledge (what in modern terms would be called the object of knowledge), but are always ways of classifying objects by means of which they are known.[29] This is what was already at stake, expressed in terms of logic, in the theory of subject and predicate. It is precisely this that is imperiled in the two-term theory and the two-name theory,

29 The point here is that universals do not have to become subjects of knowledge in order to play their predicative role in knowing, even though they can reflexively become subjects of my knowledge through a secondary act of self-knowledge. Even here, however, they are known through the act of knowing material things, as Aquinas explains: "The intellect reflects back upon itself, according to which it understands itself to understand and the species by which it understands. And so the species understood is secondarily that which is understood. But that which is understood primarily is the [external] thing of which the intelligible species is a similitude" (*ST* I 85.2). For a fuller treatment of this issue, see John P. O'Callaghan, *Thomist Realism and the Linguistic Turn* (Notre Dame, Ind.: University of Notre Dame, 2003), especially 224–27. This note and the revised sentence to which it is attached were added by the author for the English edition.

and completely forgotten in the two-class theory. In this latter theory, one no longer hesitates to describe the relationship between subject and predicate in terms of the inclu-
sion of one set within another.

The corruption of predicative logic referred to by Geach
led almost inevitably to the idea of an idea, as developed in
myriad ways by the principal authors of the
Enlightenment. It led to the reification of predicate-sub-
jects, which became mental things, yet as distinct from simple mental images. The class of objects that one predicates
of a thing thus becomes the (generic) idea of these objects.
These ideas were regarded as the mental content that *fills*
our thoughts with something. This content could even be
regarded as present in our minds from birth, as Descartes
believed, or as entirely the product of empirical investiga-
tion, as Locke maintained. Hence, a conception of intentionality, springing far more from Cartesian thought than
from the medieval notion of the *intentio*, will become the
sequel to an error of logical analysis.

According to this conception of intentionality, to know
things is to know the ideas of things, since to know is
always to apprehend that by which we represent these
things to ourselves. All our knowledge, therefore, would
rest on a preliminary examination of our own mind, by
which we each reassure ourselves of the cognitive value of
these different ideas, worthy of selection because of their
source. The modern perspective makes intentionality the
interior life of a *self* confronted with mental objects. These
objects have certain characteristics that enable us to distinguish them, describe them, and discern their interconnec-
tions. On the other hand, intentionality as St. Thomas presents it is a conceptual activity that cannot be reified because
it is entirely dispositional. It is a capacity to think singular
things in terms of concepts, linked to our ability to speak of
them.

This type of dispositionalism is clearly espoused by
Wittgenstein. After tracing a triangle, Wittgenstein affirms,

"This triangle can be seen as a triangular hole, as a solid, as a geometrical drawing; as standing on its base, as hanging from its apex; as a mountain, as a wedge, as an arrow or pointer, as an overturned object which is meant to stand on the shorter side of the right angle, as a half parallelogram, and as various other things."[30] "To see as" thus means *to see in a certain way*, to identify a singular object in terms of a certain concept. One can, of course, ask, "But how is it possible to see an object according to an *interpretation*?"[31] Wittgenstein responds, "The question represents it as a queer fact; as if something were being forced into a form it did not really fit. But no squeezing, no forcing took place here."[32] As with St. Thomas, Wittgenstein does not pose this as a question concerning the way meanings align with an exterior object, as a question concerning the correspondence between our idea of the object (material or immaterial) and the object itself about which we have an idea. We see an object because we see something about which we are able to say what it is, to classify it as a *suppositum* (the object of predication) in a sentence affirming that the object *is this* or *is that*. In other words, that it is *as* this or *as* that.

The hypostatization of predicative terms, which led to the corruption of logic, eventually gives into a further temptation: the temptation "to reduce potentialities to actualities."[33] Once again, we can marvel at how what seems so simple and clear to St. Thomas becomes so contorted for Wittgenstein, as if he is fighting to strip away erroneous Cartesian presuppositions and to escape constantly recurring internalist perspectives: to escape the ghost of a mind confronted by its own interior objects, mental objects, some of which more or less adequately represent things.

30 Ludwig Wittgenstein, *Philosophical Investigations*, II, xi, page 171.
31 Ibid.
32 Ibid.
33 Anthony Kenny, *The Metaphysics of Mind*, 73.

Intentionality and Language

Thomas and Wittgenstein do not describe the intentional life by presenting what takes place in the mind, by presenting internal operations which the thinking subject supposedly accomplishes and by means of which he or she
knows the real correlative to this intentional life. In this
regard, Descartes' conception of language is significant. In
a letter to More, dated February 5th, 1649, within the context of a comparison between machines, animals, and
humans, Descartes affirms, "Speech is the only certain sign
of thought hidden in a body."[34] Speech is a sign. It reveals
the interiority of the mind. For his part, Wittgenstein
affirms: "Misleading parallel: the expression of pain is a cry
– the expression of thought, a proposition."[35] A Cartesian
parallel that St. Thomas never makes.

In the *Disputed Questions on Truth* (14.1), while commenting on Aristotle, St. Thomas distinguishes two types
of activity in our intellect. One consists in conceiving the
simple essences of things. He explains that "in this activity,
there are found neither true nor false properly so called,
just as neither are [true and false] found in non-complex
utterances." The other activity consists in "the intellect
composing and dividing, affirming and denying, and in
this activity there is indeed found true and false, just as in
complex speech, which is its sign."[36] The term "sign" here

34 René Descartes, "To More 5 February 1649" (AT 5: 278) in *The
   Philosophical Writings of Descartes*, vol. 3, translated by J. Cottingham,
   R. Stoothoff, D. Murdock, and Anthony Kenny (Cambridge:
   Cambridge University Press, 1991), 366. On this question, see André
   Robinet, *Le Langage à l'age classique* (Paris: Klincksieck, 1978), 243–87.
35 Ludwig Wittgenstein, *Philosophical Investigations*, I §317.
36 *De Veritate* 14.1: *"intellectus enim nostri, secundum philosophum in lib. de
   anima, duplex est operatio. una qua format simplices rerum quidditates; ut
   quid est homo, vel quid est animal: in qua quidem operatione non invenitur
   verum per se et falsum, sicut nec in vocibus incomplexis. alia operatio
   intellectus est secundum quam componit et dividit, affirmando vel negando: et
   in hac iam invenitur verum et falsum, sicut et in voce complexa, quae est
   eius signum."* This text is cited by Anthony Kenny, *Aquinas* (Oxford:
   Oxford University Press, 1980), 62.

should not mislead us: it does not mean exteriorization. As Aquinas explains in his *Commentary on the De Interpretation* (1.3.26), complex understanding is a *compositio* and a *divisio*. Affirmative phrases are called a *compositio* and negative phrases a *divisio*, because they assert the existence in reality of a conjunction, in the first case, and of a separation, in the second. The difference between the two sorts of thinking occurs[37] from the difference between the use of individual words[38] and the construction of phrases. The difference between affirmative and negative judgments occurs from that between affirmative and negative phrases. As Kenny states, "this is not to be regarded as a remarkable parallelism discoverable by armchair psychology: it is simply that we have no criteria for the simplicity or complexity of thoughts other than the criteria for the simplicity or complexity of the words and sentences that give them utterance."[39]

Most of the time we are tempted to think that there is no disjunction between thought and expression. Yet, we would also like to leave open the possibility of *intuitive* thought, as Wittgenstein suggests.[40] In a sense, because of the role granted by Aquinas to the enunciation of individual words, the perspective of Aquinas can account for intuitive, even lightning-like, thought,[41] without leading him to

37 *Occurrence* is a relation between two series *A* and *B*, where *A* occurs from *B* if and only if every variation in series *A* is covariable with and depends on a variation in series *B*, without, however, this necessarily implying identity between *A* and *B*. Concerning *Occurrence* (*"survenance"*), see Roger Pouivet, "Survenances," *Critique* vol. 51, n. 575 (1995): 227–49.

38 Following Geach, we contest the popular view that the use of an isolated word does not have meaning and that it *always* presupposes, elliptically, a complete phrase. The fact that certain languages, such as Greek or Polish, have a vocative case suggests the possibility of an isolated use of a word.

39 Anthony Kenny, *Aquinas*, 63–64.

40 Ludwig Wittgenstein, *Philosophical Investigations*, I §318–20.

41 The author is alluding to Wittgenstein's expression, *"Blitzartigen Denken,"* (*Philosophical Investigations*, I §318), which Anscombe translates as "lightning-like thought." –*Trans.*

portray linguistic expression as the exteriorization of a process, which, since it is in someway instantaneous, could be dissociable from language itself. Yet, is this enough? The *Philosophical Investigations* famously contains just this type of internalist protest: "But isn't it our *meaning* it that gives sense to the sentence?" which is something private. "It is the intangible *something*; only comparable to consciousness itself. How ludicrous this might seem! It is, as it were, a dream of our language." Mischievously, Wittgenstein slips into this passage the following parenthesis: "And here, of course, belongs the fact that *one cannot mean a senseless series of words.*"[42] Wittgenstein introduces into the internalist and intuitionist cry of protest the very thing that renders it vain: the criterion of private meaning (the criterion of intentionality); what is it except a word or a series of words that usage allows, and thus *linguistic usage* itself?

For Wittgenstein, "We do not say that possibly a dog talks to itself. Is that because we are so minutely acquainted with its soul?"[43] Meaning is in a certain sense gathered from the exterior, not the interior. This insight offers a way of interpreting Aquinas' analysis that highlights the affinities between it and the view that thought is an occurrence arising from language. Thought is co-variable with and dependent on language. It is not reducible to it, because there are no psycho-linguistic laws that ensure that if someone says *this*, then he is thinking *thus*. In this sense, the language we employ is not transparent. St. Thomas knew this well. With his frequent attempts to establish the meaning of terms and to peel away the layers of meaning enwrapped within theological and philosophical propositions, Thomas was one who embraced Aristotle's constant method, the very method once again accessible to philosophy after the linguistic turn taken by Frege.[44] There is no reason to

42 Ludwig Wittgenstein, *Philosophical Investigations*, I §358. Emphasis added.
43 Ludwig Wittgenstein, *Philosophical Investigations*, I §357.
44 As Michael Dummett states: "For Frege, as for all subsequent ana-

conclude from this, however, that there is no such thing as intentionality. Intentionality operates from within one's mastery of language and not before this mastery. One can, of course, think something without saying it (to oneself) in words. Yet, what reveals the discourse to be indirect in the *that*-clause, is that we are always able to supply a linguistic expression of the thought. This applies not only to (true or false) declarative statements that take the place of x in statements of the form "someone thinks (believes, wishes, hopes, etc.) *that x*, it also applies to all forms of suspended judgment (*dubitatio*), of assertions recognizing the possibility of error (*opinio*), of beliefs not based on reasons (*fides*), as well as of statements affirming something to be true or false either on the basis of evidence (*intellectus*) or on the basis of reasons (*scientia*).[45]

The dispositional understanding of a definition amounts to knowing how to employ the word correctly, even if one is unable to give a well-crafted definition of it. To know how to employ a word is to know what it means (while being able to memorize and restate a definition does not imply that one is able to use the defined word correctly. To know what X is, to know its *quiddity*, is to be able employ the term, for example in a conversation, without the other saying to me abruptly: "but what do you *mean* by 'X'?" A child knows the quiddity of an eagle if he or she says that an eagle flies high in the sky, that it has feathers, that it has a hooked beak, and so forth. If the child says,

lytical philosophers, the philosophy of language is the foundation of all other philosophy because it is only by the analysis of language that we can analyse thought" (*Truth and Other Enigmas* [Cambridge, Mass: Harvard University Press, 1978], 442). See the opening paragraph of the *De ente et essentia*, where St. Thomas explains that, since we should avoid all ignorance of being (*ens*) and essence, "we should respond to the opening difficulty by stating what the words essence and being signify (*ad horum difficultatem aperiendam dicendum est quid nomine essentiae et entis significatur*)."

45 On this point, see *De Veritate* 14.2, and the analysis of it offered by Anthony Kenny in *Aquinas*, 64–65.

instead, that an eagle has feet like a duck, that it is covered with fur, and has a snout, I need know nothing more to affirm that the child does not know *what* an eagle is. A child, of course, does not have the knowledge of an ornithologist. Quiddities, however, as the proper objects of the first operation of the intellect (the one that does not entail *compositio* and *divisio*) *and* as the objects of the highest form of knowledge, are simultaneously the proper objects of the most basic as well as of the most sophisticated[46] intellectual knowledge (which, according to Aquinas, is itself in principle very limited).[47] The moment one speaks about something in a way that does not cause others to question his or her usage, there is clearly knowledge of a quiddity. This is not to deny, however, that the knowledge of a child differs from the knowledge of a specialist. Nor are we affirming that Thomas simply identifies a word with its quiddity. Instead, at issue here is what the correct use of a word implies: it implies the ability to think about things themselves. We do not find in Aquinas the type of positions Wittgenstein entertains only to reveal their particularly dubious character: for example, the notion that finding the proper expression of one's thoughts is comparable to a process of translation: "the thoughts are already there (perhaps were there in advance) and we merely look for their expression."[48] One's intention is to use words, but "to use words" is taken here in a very broad sense. Wittgenstein explains that "An intention is embedded in its

---

46 See Norman Kretzmann, "Philosophy of Mind," in *The Cambridge Companion to Aquinas*, edited by N. Kretzmann and E. Stump (Cambridge: Cambridge University Press, 1993), 128–59.

47 See Norman Kretzmann, "Philosophy of Mind," n. 56, p. 157, for a complete reading of the texts where St. Thomas affirms that the essential principles of things are not known. As Kenny notes, it is not clear whether for St. Thomas this limitation is a consequence of the human condition itself or merely a contingent consequence of the current state of our knowledge (see Anthony Kenny, *Aquinas*, 66.).

48 Ludwig Wittgenstein, *Philosophical Investigations*, I §335.

situation, in human customs and institutions."[49] Thus, how could I have the *intention* to say *something*, if I have not mastered the use of a language, if I have not learned it, and if I have not participated in the life of a linguistic community?

Kenny affirms that "If we want 'intellect' to mean a characteristically human capacity then it seems most helpful to regard the intellect as the capacity for thinking those thoughts that only a language-user can think."[50] Phenomenology, at least in a popularized form, has habituated us to a conception of intention that harmonizes poorly with the view that intentionality is principally exhibited in one's linguistic ability. Phenomenology is a search for the *meaning* of experience. This notion of *meaning* is no doubt directly linked to language; in many respects, Husserl justifies recourse to ideal objects by noting that they are necessary to account for the fact that we speak "of the number 2, the quality of redness, of the principle of contradiction."[51] Nevertheless, "Husserl eschews any such analysis of language, summoning it instead as witness to a 'phenomenological fact,' the existence of a mental act (the eidetic gaze) by which we all have access to what is designated."[52] To speak of *the* number 2 or of *the* apple tree presupposes a signifying intention awaiting a fulfilling intention. The famous *intentional aim* thus seems to be a sort of mental mechanism set in place once one thinks something and talks about it, as if the simple fact that one thinks about X or that one talks about X suffices for holding that there is

---

49 Ibid., I §337.
50 Anthony Kenny, *Aquinas*, 67.
51 Edmond Husserl, *Logical Investigations*, translated by J. N. Findlay (New York: Humanities Press, 1970), II §8, vol. 1, page, 352. See Vincent Descombes, *Objects of All Sorts: A Philosophical Grammar*, translated by Lorna Scott-Fox and Jeremy Harding (Baltimore: Johns Hopkins University Press, 1986), 49–61.
52 Vincent Descombes, *Objects of All Sorts: A Philosophical Grammar*, 56.

a fact for a consciousness to think and for a subject to speak. Husserl, in section 131 of *Ideas* – which Descombes describes as the place where we witness "the disaster, no less, of Husserlian phenomenology"[53] – refers to the intended object as offering itself to me as the meaning of a certain object, such as the apple tree in the garden. The meaning, the ensemble of appearances, is distinct from the object. Yet, it must also be identical to it, if the intended object is truly the apple tree. It is "the *'object'* [*'Gegenstand'*], the *'Object'* [*'Objekt'*], the *'Identical,'* the 'determinable subject of its possible predicates' – *the pure X in abstraction from all predicates* – and it becomes separated *from* these predicates or, more precisely, from the predicate-noemas."[54] We understand what it means to say that *x* is identical to *y*, but what does it mean to say that it is both the "identical" as well as the "object" [*"Gegenstand"*]? How could an object remain after all its predicates have been abstracted from it? How could the meaning of our experiences have any relation to this *"pure X"*? The Phenomenologists, it is true, offer responses to such questions. They bring to light, after peeling the onion a little more deeply, a new foundational layer of meaning that we should take into account. Fundamentally, all things and all types of things are *essentially* associated to a certain type of intentional experience, in other words, to a subjective aiming. They cannot be *given* except in this way. By this means we avoid the naïve descriptions of experience offered by stale philosophies that merely study language (the only signifying modality in our relation to the object) without taking into account the other perceptive and imaginative modalities, modalities

53 Ibid., 57.
54 Edmond Husserl, *Ideas Pertaining to a Pure Phenomenology and to a Phenomenological Philosophy, First Book: General Introduction to a Pure Phenomenology*, Edmund Husserl *Collected Works*, Vol. 2, translated by F. Kersten (The Hague: Martinus Nijhoff Publishers, 1982), §131, page 313.

upon which the properly linguistic modality can build. Yet, as Descombes states,

> How is the difference between one experience (seeing Venice, for instance) and another (imagining it) synonymous with the difference between the meaning of the first and that of the second if not because it is the difference between the meaning of the statement relating the first and that of the statement relating the second? But then the real given is not a totality of lived states. It is a totality of ways of speaking.[55]

This is why to find a phenomenology of intentionality we should turn not to Husserl but to Wittgenstein – to him who can, "after a fashion be considered as the anti-Husserl."[56] As Descombes explains, "the description of a mental act is a description of the language of this act."[57] We should interpret "language" here as referring to the many practices tied to linguistic usage, practices which Wittgenstein never tired of considering.

The end of the internalist parenthesis affects not only Cartesianism, but the whole phenomenological movement. A retrospective reading of Aquinas that interprets him in light of Wittgenstein undermines the entire project of the philosophy of knowledge considered as first philosophy (especially the study of perception as experienced by a consciousness). This reading affects Husserl's thought just as much as Descartes'. After Frege, this undermining becomes the primary and newly recognized role of logic and grammar. Henceforth, St. Thomas becomes much more intelligible. His analysis of intentionality no longer seems inadequate because pre-Husserlian (which is how the Phenomenologists read him), but acquires the character of a survivor who has escaped the dangers, so to speak, of phenomenology.

---

55 Vincent Descombes, *Objects of All Sorts: A Philosophical Grammar*, 59.
56 Jacques Bouveresse, *Le mythe de l'intériorité*, iv.
57 Vincent Descombes, *Objects of All Sorts: A Philosophical Grammar*, 59.

The Intentional Object

The theory of the intentional object, which plays such a paramount role in phenomenology generally, creates the greatest obstacle to understanding the Thomistic conception of intentionality. In acts of consciousness, we would be conscious of an object, whether or not an object actually exists. Intentionality becomes a phenomenological property of consciousness. This thesis, at least in its Husserlian idealist form, seems to lie at the heart of many aberrations.[58] An article by Elizabeth Anscombe entitled, "The Intentionality of Sensation,"[59] brings these assertions to light and leads us back to St. Thomas and Wittgenstein.

Anscombe discerns two distinct conceptions of the intentional object: one new, one old. In the old one, the *subject* is the real thing existing independently of the conception we have of it; the *object* is the *object of*. In other words, it is an object *of* perception, *of* thought, *of* desire, and so on. In this sense, the object is not an object that we could find somewhere, however we might envision it, even (and still less) as something *in* our consciousness. As Anscombe explains, "The *realitas objectiva* of an idea thus meant what we should call its 'content' – namely what it is of, but considered as belonging purely to the idea."[60] The phrase, "what it is of" has two senses. In the first, it signifies the model (the subject); in the second, it refers to what is included in the idea (the object), which might not even resemble the original model (subject). If we were to say

58 The doubts raised above concerning the adequacy of the foundation from which phenomenological analysis generally proceeds does not prevent us from recognizing that the work of Husserl and other Phenomenologists provide a fascinating analysis of the limitations of certain fundamental concepts, such as *act*, *content*, and *object*.

59 Elizabeth Anscombe, "The Intentionality of Sensation: a Grammatical Feature," in *Metaphysics and the Philosophy of Mind, Collected Philosophical Papers II* (Minneapolis: University of Minnesota Press, 1981), 3–20.

60 Ibid., 3.

here that there could be an object of desire even when the object of this desire does not exist – that it is not necessary for there to be an object that one desires when there is an object of desire – we would be employing *confusedly* the two above mentioned senses of the phrase "what it is of." This would be a strange question, since to ask whether the intentional object exists *makes no sense*. An object is an object of something, of perception, of thought, of desire; the problem of its existence or non-existence never arises. It is not a *subject*, which can exist or not exist. Anscombe, there-fore, offers a precision: "Now to prevent confusion I will introduce the phrase 'intentional object' to mean 'object' in the older sense which still occurs in 'object of desire.'"[61]

How does this differ from a phenomenological analysis? It differs because the word "intention" is employed here according to its standard meaning as commonly used in human action (as in "he has the intention of coming tomor-row morning"). Many of the concepts marked by inten-tionality, in other words, those that appear in descriptions of an action as intentional, are verbs that take direct objects. Once again, this does not imply that *intentional entities* actu-ally exist, but only that intentional objects, as defined above, exist.[62] "Obvious examples of intentional verbs are 'to think of', 'to worship', 'to shoot at.'"[63] With verbs of this sort, we are led to attribute intentional characteristics to the action related to the object that follows the verb. Anscombe recognizes that "'Thinking of' is a verb for which the topic of the non-existent object is full of traps and temptations."[64] Nonetheless, it is not possible to assimilate expressions such as "X worships Y" and "X thinks of Y" to "X hits Y." In "X hits Y," we should be able put the name of some real-ly existing person (of a subject as defined above) in the

61 Ibid., 4.
62 For the difference between intentional entities and intentional objects, see the glossary at the end of this volume.
63 Elizabeth Anscombe, "The Intentionality of Sensation," 4.
64 Ibid.

place of Y, which is not necessarily the case in the expressions "X worships Y" and "X thinks of Y" (where Y could be Zeus or a unicorn). A large part of the problem comes from the fact that if Y in "X thinks of Y" is something real, it is the real thing that is under consideration, and not an intermediary, which is what the earlier critiqued representationalist perspective would like to suggest. Consequently, when in the place of Y there is a *vacuous* name, the name of a fictional entity, the temptation is to think of it as some sort of peculiar intentional or intensional[65] reality (a noema, a pure intensional content), the correlate of an intentional act or aim.[66] The characteristic feature of internalist philosophers would thus be that they never truly consider whether the issue of intentionality simply concerns a *grammatical* possibility: the possibility of using correctly a verb that need not be followed by the name of a subject, but that might very well be followed by the name of an intentional object. Nevertheless, we do not say that X worships an idea or an intentional object. The phrase that describes what X does (worship) in no way presupposes for its truth that "worship" be followed by the name of a subject. On the other hand, "hit" must be followed by the name of a subject for the phrase "X hits Y" not to be false.

Intentionality is not a property of acts of consciousness; it concerns the description of what people do: they think of, they worship, they shoot at, and so forth. Intentionality is not an internal operation presupposing layers of constitutive meaning – presupposing an "egological" life that science might one day be able to delineate. Instead, intention-

65 For the distinction between intentional and intensional, see "intensional" in the glossary. For a deliberately non-intensionalist (or even non-intentionalist) theory of fiction, see Roger Pouivet, *Esthétique et logique* (Liège: Mardaga, 1996).

66 "Noema" is the second half of the conceptual pair "noesis/noema" introduced by Edmund Husserl in *Ideas* (*First Book* §88–§94). "Noesis" is the act of consciousness, while the "noema" is object of that consciousness. *–Trans.*

ality concerns the way someone – who is simply able to answer the question, "whom do the Greeks worship?" – describes what the Greeks do. Elizabeth Anscombe explains that "an intentional object is given by a word or a phrase that gives *a description under which*."[67] It is because of this that one cannot detach the notion itself of intentionality (as a relationship between what one thinks and that about which one thinks) from a description of that about which one thinks when one thinks it, because it is exactly *about it* that one is thinking.

This conception of intentionality, which does not detach it from the question of knowing how to describe what someone thinks, helps us understand better the (celebrated) passage in which Thomas explains that "the likeness of the visible thing is that by which sight sees, and the likeness of the intelligible thing, which is the intelligible species, is the form by which the intellect knows."[68] What does St. Thomas want to say? That the salt and my capacity to recognize the salt resemble each other? Certainly not. On the contrary, the description of the content of the idea and that of the subject of the idea, in one way resemble each other. "For instance," Kenny explains, "the idea that the world will shortly come to an end might be said to be the idea of a certain state of affairs: to specify *which* idea is involved one uses exactly the same expression 'that the world will shortly come to an end.'"[69] The description under which one thinks something or thinks that something is this or that, is not different from the description of that about which one thinks or what one thinks concerning something. What St. Thomas wanted to say through the scholastic language of forms and likenesses is that the reality known is known through the description of the

67 Elizabeth Anscombe, "The Intentionality of Sensation," 9.
68 *ST* I 85.2: "*similitudo rei visibilis est secundum quam visus videt; et similitudo rei intellectae, quae est species intelligibilis, est forma secundum quam intellectus intelligit.*"
69 Anthony Kenny, *Aquinas*, 72.

intentional object expressed in such phrases as "*X* thinks that *Y*," or "*X* worships *Y*."

In the *Philosophical Grammar*, Wittgenstein states that, "In the proposition, 'I believe that *P* is the case' we feel that the essential thing, the real process of belief, isn't expressed but only hinted at; we feel it must be possible to replace this hint by a description of the mechanism of belief."[70] This feeling corresponds *grosso modo* to Husserl's phenomenological project. This project rests upon the idea that we miss what is essential if we fail to describe the intentional acts of consciousness. Consciousness is what gives life to the phenomenon of intentionality itself. Certain phenomenologists would probably be convinced that we have missed the *meaning*, if we say that we can express it simply through a particular language, with all its contingencies, and that there is nothing beyond the description by means of which we describe, not interior acts, but behaviors (to worship) or thoughts (*X* thinks that). Nevertheless, as with Wittgenstein, St. Thomas never seemed to have the slightest interest in examining the interior processes constitutive of the meaning of what we say, nor, in general, in probing the modalities of our representations of the real.

Wittgenstein again remarks that:

> When we intend, we exist among the pictures (shadows) of intention, as well as with real things. Let us imagine we are sitting in a darkened cinema and entering into the happenings in the film. Now the lights are turned on, though the film continues on the screen. But suddenly we see it "from outside" as movements of light and dark patches on a screen.[71]

The intentional object is nothing other than the expression that follows the intentional verb. In a sense, it is a series of words, as the film is a movement of light and dark patches on a screen. Yet, no one will want to say this, because the

70 Ludwig Wittgenstein, *Philosophical Grammar*, part 1, n. 63, p. 104.
71 Ibid., part 1, n. 98, p. 146.

intentional object so conceived is "without life and of no interest to us."[72] The mythology of interiority, however, adds nothing but mystery, because there is nothing more than a movement of light and shadow on a screen, a series of words that follow verbs used in this or that way. The theory that when I think of a cow or that there is a cow in the meadow, I have *in esse intentionale* the form of the cow in my mind, could seem phenomenologically extremely simplistic; but if Aquinas wants to say by this that I know how to use the word "cow" or the expression containing this word such that we can describe what I'm doing when I say that I think of a cow or that there is a cow in the meadow, then the thesis that the form *in esse naturale* and *in esse intentionale* are alike becomes much less crude. To know the reality of something by means of the likeness of its form is simply to be able to speak intelligibly about it.

The Intentionality of Perception

St. Thomas also states that "the likeness of the visible thing is that by which sight sees."[73] This time, how can we still say with Wittgenstein that "It is *in language* that it's all done"?[74] Elizabeth Anscombe, however, does not hesitate to say that the verbs of sense perception are intentional verbs, or at least that they have an essentially intentional aspect.[75] This is particularly the case with "to see." We see the table or we see that the table has been set. Thomas insists that,

> Sense images are not able to modify the possible [receptive] intellect, but must be rendered actually intelligible by the agent intellect [i.e., the active intellect as a producer of concepts]. Thus, sense cognition cannot be said to be the total and perfect cause of

---

72 Ibid.
73 *ST* I 85.2: "*similitudo rei visibilis est secundum quam visus videt.*"
74 Ludwig Wittgenstein, *Philosophical Grammar*, part 1, n. 95, p. 143.
75 Elizabeth Anscombe, "The Intentionality of Sensation," 11.

intellectual cognition, but rather in a certain way its material cause.[76]

This means that it is not possible to isolate an original, primary, and infra-conceptual moment of sensation, a moment in which the conceptual, and hence linguistic, capacity is not exercised. In the interpretive framework proposed here, the intentional character of verbs of sense perception indicate that we remain still and always in the domain of language. Concerning sight, Thomas explains, following one tradition, that sight is the sense we know best, "because it is less material."[77] Knowledge presupposes that he who knows has the form of the thing in an immaterial way. There is no reason to think, if we follow Thomas, that the form – in other words the quiddity or the capacity to use a word or phrase intelligibly – is less involved in perception than in any activities that engage the senses less. To say that perception is intentional, therefore, is to note that the sensible and the intelligible are not opposed to each other in St. Thomas any more than they are in contemporary *non-phenomenological* theories (such as Rudolf Arnheim's theory, for example).[78] With regard to these contemporary theories, Jacques Bouveresse states that the tendency "will be to hold instead that all reputedly higher

---

76 *ST* I 84.6: *"phantasmata non sufficiunt immutare intellectum possibilem, sed oportet quod fiant intelligibilia actu per intellectum agentem; non potest dici quod sensibilis cognitio sit totalis et perfecta causa intellectualis cognitionis, sed magis quodammodo est materia causae."*

77 *ST* I 84.2: *"quia est minus materialis."* See also *ST* I 78.3.

78 Rudolf Arnheim (1904–) is a Berlin trained psychologist and immigrant to the United States who has applied Gestalt theory to the study of art. He has also attempted to develop a renewed conception of cognition. See R. Arnheim, *Art and Visual Perception* (Berkeley: University of California Press, 1954) and R. Arnheim, *Visual Thinking* (Berkeley: University of California Press, 1969). For a study of the work of this centenarian, see Ian Verstegen, "The Thought, Life and Influence of Rudolf Arnheim," in *Genetic, Social and General Psychological Monographs* (Washington, D.C.: Heldref, 1996), vol. 122, pages 197–213. *–Trans.*

intellectual functions that apparently require the assistance of consciousness are already at work in perception itself, even, as some would say, in animals."[79]

The issue of attributing to animals such a properly active capacity in perception itself is important. If such a capacity is linked to language, then clearly there will be no question of attributing it to animals. When I say that the dog sees that the table is set or that the sea rises, I am not ready to ascribe to him the intentional state that I would attribute to a human being. We might even question whether I would ever say that the dog sees such things. I would say that he sees that his bowl is full because he rushes toward it; I would say that he sees his master arrive because he jumps and barks happily, and so on. Yet, would I say of a dog that he sees a splendid sunset? As Wittgenstein remarks, "only of a living human being and what resembles (behaves like) a living human being can one say: it has sensations; it sees; is blind; hears; is deaf; is conscious or unconscious."[80] Without doubt, St. Thomas would say the same thing. This indicates that perception should be understood as intentional. It retains an intrinsic relationship with the expressions that follow verbs of perception and renders intelligible our ability to say of someone that "she sees this," or that "she sees that." We might attribute to an animal, such as a dog or a cat, certain physiological and behavioral traits analogous to those of humans. We might say this of a dog or a cat, but not of a cockroach or a leech. To say that "the cockroach saw you come over to him in order to squish him" makes no sense, and not merely because of the perceptual apparatus of the cockroach.

In the *Zettel*, Wittgenstein states,

79 Jacques Bouveresse, *Langage, perception et réalité* (Nîmes: J. Chambon, 1995), 402.
80 Ludwig Wittgenstein, *Philosophical Investigations*, I §281. Concerning this issue, see the chapter entitled "the Homunculus Fallacy" (ch. 9) in Anthony Kenny, *The Legacy of Wittgenstein*, 125–36.

"What I perceive is *this* – " and now follows a form of *description*. The word "this" might also be explained as follows: "let us imagine a direct transfer of experience." – But now what is our criterion for the experience's really having been transferred? "Well, he just does have what I have." – But how does *he* "*have*" *it*?[81]

To have this perception is to have *this*, but what will *this* be except that description? For example, what would be the directly transferred internal experience of seeing red? Without doubt, if someone were to say "it's red," no one would deny it. Clearly, one does not decide by consensus whether he or she sees red. Yet, how could an experience of seeing red be totally independent of such a properly linguistic consensus concerning whether *red* is truly the color that applies in this case? Wittgenstein adds that, "The description of what is subjectively seen is more or less akin to the description of an object, but just for that reason does not function as a description of an object."[82] This reinforces the notion that to see this or that does not consist in being a spectator of an internal spectacle, something that one observes in oneself or about oneself. There is indeed, therefore, a difference between seeing and observing, but not to such an extent that sight would be anything else than seeing *such and such*, in other words, than seeing it *under a certain description*. According to Elizabeth Anscombe, this is exactly what intentionality is.[83]

To say with St. Thomas that "the likeness of the visible thing is that by which sight sees" also enable us to recognize the well-known example of the rabbit/duck sketch, which one either sees as an image of a duck or of a rabbit, but never as both at the same time.[84] Let us suppose that person *A* sees a duck, while person *B* sees a rabbit. Clearly

81 Ludwig Wittgenstein, *Zettel*, §433.
82 Ludwig Wittgenstein, *Zettel*, §435.
83 Elizabeth Anscombe, "The Intentionality of Sensation," 9.
84 See Ludwig Wittgenstein, *Philosophical Investigations*, II, xi, page 166, which contains the sketch.

it would be absurd to say that they *in fact* see the same thing, because when asked one will say he sees a rabbit, while the other will say a duck. Some have suggested that we must therefore distinguish sensation from perception, and say that if their visual sensations are the same, their perceptions are different.[85] Yet, as Wittgenstein asks concerning a similar example, "what is the 'it' which I see now this way, now that? Is it the drawing? And how do I know it is the same drawing both times? Do I merely know this, or do I *see* it as well?"[86] As Jacques Bouveresse explains, "The question posed here . . . is to know how it happens that we can use the interpretation as a description of what was immediately perceived and at the same time affirm that this description is only 'indirect.'"[87] What the interpretation adds to what is immediately perceived cannot be perceived, nor can that to which the interpretation is added. We are thus tempted to say with Thomas that the form is there, even when there could be several of them (a rabbit or a duck) to the extent that "sense images not [being] able to modify the possible intellect, [they] must be rendered actually intelligible by the agent intellect."[88] In Thomas Aquinas' philosophy of knowledge, the study of perception does not presuppose that we isolate a moment of perception or of sense, from which flow the higher intellectual operations, as certain empiricist philosophers affirm, with their theories of sense data and impressions. As Joseph Moreau states,

> we see from this what the celebrated Aristotelian definition of sensation means: the common act of the sen-

85 This position is held today by Jean-Pierre Changeux, *Neuronal Man: the Biology of the Mind* (New York: Pantheon Books, 1985), 130–34.
86 Ludwig Wittgenstein, *Remarks on the Philosophy of Psychology*, vol. I, §31.
87 Jacques Bouveresse, *Langage, perception et réalité*, 339.
88 *ST* I 84.6: "*phantasmata non sufficiunt immutare intellectum possibilem, sed oportet quod fiant intelligibilia actu per intellectum agentem.*"

sible and the sensing; it is best understood as an effort to overcome a sensualist perspective, without escaping into idealism, into a transcendental idealism for which cognitive determinations can only come from the intellect.[89]

Knowledge does indeed differ according to whether one remains on the level of simple sense apprehension or on the level of reason; nevertheless, there is never a moment when the properly human linguistic capacity does not play a decisive role. This is what it means to say that it is the man who perceives and not a thinking substance or a faculty – of sense or even of consciousness – effecting vigorous syntheses on appearances that seem never truly to attain anything but appearances.

These remarks are not meant to solve the problems raised, especially the problem of intentionality. The goal has been to show that both Descartes and Husserl presuppose a conception of interiority that Saint Thomas, to his great good fortune, never knew, and from which Wittgenstein, by means of his disconcerting philosophical detours, succeeded in disentangling himself (and us).

89 Joseph Moreau, *De la connaissance selon saint Thomas d'Aquin* (Paris: Beauchesne, 1976), 14.

CHAPTER FIVE
THE WILL

To call into question internalism (the thesis according to which the ultimate justification of our beliefs rests upon the notion that each person has a privileged relationship with his own mind) does not merely concern knowledge of the external world. We can also pursue our critique of internalism in a domain common to ethics and to the philosophies of mind and of action: in the domain described as the philosophy of will.

In an article dedicated to Descartes' theory of the will, Anthony Kenny compares what Descartes says about the will in *The Rules for the Direction of the Mind* with what he says about it in the *Meditations* and subsequently.[1] Descartes removes from the understanding the power to affirm or deny – in other words, the power to judge – and accords it to the will itself. In his letter to Mesland of 9 February 1645, he affirms that "it is always open to us to hold back from pursuing a clearly known good, or from admitting a clearly perceived truth, provided we consider it a good thing to demonstrate the freedom of our will by so doing."[2] Descartes clearly envisages a form of autonomy

1   Anthony Kenny, "Descartes on the Will," in R. J. Butler, ed., *Cartesian Studies* (Oxford: Blackwell, 1972), 1–31; reprinted in Anthony Kenny, *The Anatomy of the Soul: Historical Essays in the Philosophy of Mind* (Oxford: Blackwell, 1973), 81–112.

in the will: the will affirms and denies. Now, we can distinguish in any phrase between what Richard M. Hare calls its descriptive content (the *phrastic*) and the mode of expression (the *neustic*): how the content that one asserts is asserted.[3] According to Kenny's interpretation, Descartes considers that understanding only concerns contents, independent of their modalities (affirmative or negative). An affirmative judgment would involve the will to the extent that the will joins to the content (the *phrastic*) a neustic, namely an affirmation.[4] Descartes also thinks that human understanding, when one uses it correctly, is infallible. Every erroneous judgment, therefore, must be a (moral) fault, consisting either in affirming what the intellect does not know or in contradicting what it does know.

The Myth of Volitions

If we distinguish between the *phrastic* (the content of a phrase) and its *neustic*, then the *neustic* – whether it be an affirmation or a negation, or an imperative with all its possible nuances, from "could you be so good as to close the door" to "the door!" – can easily seem to arise from and be the linguistic expression of a particular faculty. The expression of a wish or of a command, perhaps even more than an affirmation or negation, would thus bear witness to an interior event: volition. Ryle affirms that his goal is "to refute the doctrine that there exists a Faculty, immaterial Organ, or Ministry, corresponding to the theory's description of the 'Will' and, accordingly, that there occur processes, or operations, corresponding to what it describes as 'volitions.'"[5] There is no question here, however, of con-

---

2 René Descartes, "To Mesland of 9 February 1645" (AT 4: 173) in *The Philosophical Writings of Descartes*, v. 3, p. 245.
3 Richard M. Hare, *The Language of Morals* (Oxford: Clarendon Press, 1952), §2.1, pp. 17–20.
4 This thesis is rejected by Frege, for whom a negation is an assertion having a negative meaning, and not an indifferent content to which one joins a negative neustic.

testing the distinction between actions that are voluntary and those that are not; or even of denying the distinction between vigorous acts and acts that lack will. It is simply that we should avoid falling into the metaphorical trap set by expressions such as the ones we have just employed: "lack of will" is not the absence of *something* that would be the will.

If we were to say that someone voluntarily pulled the trigger of a gun, we might suppose, according to a general conception of the will promoted by modern philosophy, that a volition is the *cause* of the fact that someone has pulled the trigger. We should note, however, that "Novelists describe the actions, remarks, gestures and grimaces, the daydreams, deliberations, qualms and embarrassments of their characters; but they never mention their volitions. They would not know what to say about them."[6] To say that someone wants something, we do not speak about his will, we speak about something else: specifically, about a certain way he has of acting. True, one could object that the will, as the source of volitions, is concealed from everyone else except the one who has this will. Internalism recognizes not only that the volitions of others are always inferred from their acts, but also that everyone has by himself direct access to his own volitions. But this explains nothing. If I interpret the behavior of an individual as intentional (that he wants to do what he does, such as pull the trigger), it is by describing his behavior in terms of intentionality, saying that if he pulls the trigger it is because

5   Gilbert Ryle, *The Concept of Mind* (London: Hutchinson, 1949), 63.
6   Ibid., 64. On this point, see Vincent Descombes, *Proust, philosophie du roman* (Paris: Ed. de Minuit, 1987) in which the author shows how Proust embraces almost all the dogmas of internalist philosophy (private language, interiority, the virtual impossibility of communication, idealism, abstractionism, self-expression, etc.). When, however, Proust writes *Remembrance of Things Past (In Search of Lost Time)*, he does something entirely different, because "the novel portrays every event from the perspective of its being an action in which several characters participate" (p. 19) and thus constructs *descriptions* of attitudes and not testimonies of the content of thought.

he wants to pull it. Volitions play no role in the explanation of behavior in terms of intentionality. Nor does the absence of volition play any part in the explanation of the mechanism of the trigger, by which the movement of one piece of the gun leads to the firing of the bullet. In this last case, a description in terms of intentionality is simply out of the question.

With respect to the supposed direct access to volitions, we can note that no one ever observes his or her own volitions. Instead, we speak of our actions – past, present, and future – in terms of intentionality. The fact that first-person discourse is irreducible to second- or third-person discourse, the fact that we can hide our wishes and our wills, or that we can even discover them by thinking about what we do or would like to do: here again, these all pertain to the description of our behavior; they do not imply that we grasp volitions as particular mental events taking place in the foreground of consciousness. Key here is the dispositional character of the notion of will, and not any particular episode that supposedly is the interior cause of what one does. Paradoxically, it was because we tried to apply to the specification of our acts the causal structure proper to our description of non-intentional mechanisms (such as the trigger mechanism of a firearm) that the myth of volitions was able to arise.

One could object that the "myth of volitions" is itself mythic, because no philosopher has ever asserted the existence of volitions conceived of as interior events that cause our actions and render them voluntary. Granted that with the advent Descartes the role attributed to the will in the voluntarist tradition developed by moral philosophy during the Middle Ages appears in a new light, there can be no question here of ascribing voluntarism to Descartes himself.[7] The point, however, is not to affirm that Descartes himself held *such* a thesis. Instead, the point is that the

7   This critique could be leveled at Ryle and Kenny when they stigmatize the (supposed) thesis of the phantom in the machine. Is it not

Cartesian conception, at least in its popular form, suggested this thesis to a whole tradition of "reflexive" philosophy.[8] *Mutatis mutandis*, such a conception is affirmed also by Kant.

In the celebrated passage from the *Groundwork of the Metaphysics of Morals*, Kant states: "It is impossible to think of anything at all in the world, or indeed even beyond it, that could be considered good without limitation except a *good will*."[9] The will is understood here as an internal reality, the real cause of our moral actions. It is significant that for Kant, "Moderation in affects and passions, self-control, and calm reflection"[10] are not good without restriction ("however unconditionally they were praised by the ancients"),[11] but only in relation to the principles of a good will. A Kantian will say that it is precisely the autonomy of the will that is decisive. For Kant, "The principle of autonomy is, therefore: to choose only in such a way that the maxims of your choice are also included as universal law in the same volition."[12] Yet, what is an act of willing but a volition? An autonomous volition, isn't this a volition whose rule is universalizable? From this perspective, an act is

here a question of a phantom of a phantom? In other words, did Descartes really hold such a thesis, at least in such a crude from?

8   This "reflexive" philosophy is overwhelmingly dominant in academic (i.e., not scholastic) philosophy in France. Descartes is thus the philosopher of the "discovery" of subjectivity as foundational, a discovery that will subsequently be exploited by Kant and later by Husserl.

9   Immanuel Kant, *Groundwork of the Metaphysics of Morals*, translated and edited by Mary Gregor (Cambridge: Cambridge University Press, 1997), 7 (AK 4:393). Except for *The Critique of Pure Reason*, the citation method used for quotations from Kant's works is the following: after the page number of the Cambridge edition, the volume number followed by the page number of the standard German edition from the German Academy is given in parentheses (AK stands for *akademie*). –*Trans.*

10   Ibid., 8 (AK 4:394).

11   Ibid.

12   Ibid., 47 (AK 4:440).

moral not because it is virtuous[13] or because it has benefi-
cial consequences, but because it results from an uncondi-
tioned cause, being autonomous on the level of its own
principle. The will is thus understood as producing volitions. Heteronomy, on the other hand, occurs when "the
will . . . does not give itself the law; instead the object, by
means of its relation to the will, gives the law to it."[14] The
will must search for the law. It will find it in itself and will
then will as it should will. For Kant, what is important is
not that a *person* wills what he should, as he should, when
he should, but that a will produce these volitions in complete autonomy. These volitions do not even presuppose an
end to be achieved,[15] but merely the rational subject existing by itself.

If we agree to speak of the will as an internal reality that
generates our morality and is virtually separate from specific types of human behavior, then we agree to regard the
will as a protagonist capable of autonomy, of having its
own maxims and laws. The issue becomes no longer
whether someone shows that he or she has a will. Instead,
we are essentially led to portray the will itself as a type of
agent.[16] The atmosphere here is entirely different from the
one we find with Aquinas when he states that "since man
both excels at knowing the end of his acts and at moving
himself to act, it is in his acts that the voluntary is princi-

13 Virtuous in the sense of the cardinal virtues as interpreted by St.
   Thomas in *ST* II-II 47–170. See also Elizabeth Anscombe's classic article, "Modern Moral Philosophy," *Philosophy* 33 (1958): 1–19; reprinted in *Virtue Ethics*, edited by Roger Crisp and Michael Slote (Oxford:
   Oxford University Press, 1997), 26–44; see as well, Peter Geach, *The
   Virtues* (Cambridge: Cambridge University Press, 1977).
14 Immanuel Kant, *Groundwork of the Metaphysics of Morals*, 47 (AK
   4:441).
15 Such an end "would make every will only relatively good" (Ibid., 44
   [AK 4:437]).
16 Kant's use of the term "person" is as *disincarnated* as the use of the
   term will. According to Kant, the person is not properly any particular person.

pally found."[17] It is the human person, this man here or that man there, who acts when doing what he should or shouldn't, and not some philosophical entity, the will, whether autonomous or not. In place of the term "atmosphere" we could prefer the term *tradition*, defined as a specific set of concepts and principles of justification, having its proper coherence, and in which certain problems are intelligible and others hardly so or even not at all.[18]

Can We Observe Willing?

If volitions are really psychological events that possess causal power and that we can observe within us, then voluntary actions are caused merely by the will and free actions are those in which volitions presuppose no other antecedent cause than the will itself (a good will). Yet, is it possible to hold that one can formulate interiorly a representation of the will through introspection? This portrayal of one's ability to apprehend one's own will as the causal source of what one wants presupposes that each of us is a sort of spectator before our own wills. To will would rest upon our ability to perceive that we want and to will what we want: to will to will. Besides the patently infinite regression that this view entails, we can note along with Wittgenstein that "when I raise my arm 'voluntarily' I do not use any instrument to bring the movement about. My wish is not such an instrument either."[19] These volitions are not the means by which we will, the means by which we command ourselves: "As if, that is, the will were an influence, a force, or again: a primary *action*, which then is the cause of the outward perceptible action."[20]

If willing does not stop at the moment of action, it is

---

17 *ST* I-II 6.1: "*cum homo maxime cognoscat finem sui operis et moveat seipsum, in eius actibus maxime voluntarium invenitur.*"
18 Concerning this notion of tradition, see Alasdair MacIntyre, *Whose Justice? Which Rationality?* (Notre Dame, Ind.: University of Notre Dame Press, 1988), 1–11.
19 Ludwig Wittgenstein, *Philosophical Investigations*, I §614.
20 Ludwig Wittgenstein, *Remarks on the Philosophy of Psychology*, vol. I,

probably not merely that which initiates the action. It is the action itself. Willing is not what makes us speak, write, walk, or lift something: willing is speaking, writing, walking, and lifting without our being constrained to do so. Willing is not something that occurs *antecedently*, in the secret of our minds as a private event. Wittgenstein explains, "one might say: voluntary movement is marked by the absence of surprise. And now I do not mean you to ask 'But *why* isn't one surprised here?'"[21] Wittgenstein acknowledges that,

> One sometimes says: "What was I going to look for in this drawer? – Oh yes, the photograph!" Once this has occurred to us, we recall the connexion between our actions and what was happening before. But the following is also possible: I open the drawer and routle around in it; at last I come to and ask myself "Why am I rummaging in this drawer?" And then the answer comes, "I want to look at the photograph of . . ." "*I want to*," not "*I wanted to*." Opening the drawer, etc. happened so to speak automatically and got interpreted subsequently.[22]

In order to account for what happened, it is not necessary that I turn to an interior region. There is little chance of my being surprised that I wanted to search the drawer, even though I might not now remember why I am doing so. This would simply mean that I no longer have the intention to search it, that I no longer understand what I am doing, and not that I lost interior contact with my volition. My will cannot be understood except in the context of what I do, as interpreted (after the fact) by me or by someone else. To recover my awareness of what I wanted is not like interior-

§900. See also *Remarks on the Philosophy of Psychology*, vol. II, §78, 122. According to Kant, the application of the categorical imperative presupposes a primary phase in which I pass possible actions through the crucible of the criterion of universalizability to know if they are *willed* in the moral sense of a good will.
21 Ludwig Wittgenstein, *Philosophical Investigations*, I §628.
22 Ludwig Wittgenstein, *Zettel*, §8.

ly recovering a lost item, as when someone finds his keys by fortuitously stumbling upon them. To recover this awareness is to continue doing what one was doing with the knowledge of *why* one is doing it: in other words, to be able once again to give a teleological description (in terms of a final cause) of what one is doing.[23]

As often happens during the course of Wittgenstein's analysis, a particular philosophical conception begins to appear mythic from the moment we consider the way we learned to do the very thing the philosophical conception is meant to explain. The myth of volitions presupposes that we learned to perceive that we will something by grasping the interior acts that cause what we do. A child, however, does not voluntarily or involuntary learn to will or to play. What leads him to will – for him as for anyone else – is what happens when he does something, the character of his actions, the consequences they bring.[24] He knows that he wills not because he has finally pinpointed the volitions in his mind, but because of what he does and says when he does or says this or that. The child learns to will, not in the sense of learning to have volitions, but by mastering certain situations, which, as he grows older, become increasingly complex. It is from within such situations that we attribute a will to someone. Not to respond when we call you reveals your ill will: it reveals that you do not want to respond. When a child does not come when called, we might ask him: "do you not want to come?" (Clearly, we would not ask him: "do you not find this volition within yourself?) He learns what "not wanting to" means by hearing his own attitude described as not wanting to.

Wittgenstein explains that, "One draws quite different conclusions from an involuntary movement and from a voluntary: this *characterizes* voluntary movement."[25] The

23 Peter Geach offers an analysis of teleological explanation in "Teleological Explanation," in *Explanation*, edited by Stephen Körner (New Haven, Conn.: Yale University Press, 1975), 76–95.
24 Ludwig Wittgenstein, *Zettel*, §587.

error of the modern conception of the will is to have understood the will as *the cause* of our voluntary actions, instead
of understanding it as *constitutive* of our voluntary
actions.[26] To explain a voluntary action by saying that it is
caused by a volition, by a certain psychological event recognized as such by the subject of this state, is to apply
(apply badly) a causal model. The proper explanation of
the voluntary character of an action, however, does not
belong to this order of things. A proper explanation presupposes that we describe action in a certain way and that
we do not envision describing it in any other way, unless
we accede to offering an inadequate description of it. An
adequate explanation does not take for granted that volitions are the causes of our actions. An action is voluntary
because it is a certain type of action, directed toward a (teleological) end and thus presupposing certain types of
beings capable of such goal-directed action, and not
because it has an internal, reflexive, and volitional cause.
The will is less the name of a type of internal causality
proper to a certain faculty, than a disposition attributed to
beings whose actions can be described in a certain way, for
example, in a way that would not be appropriate to a
description of a stone, nor extendable to a dog except ana-
logically.

Kant's questions concerning the morality of a person's
acts does not focus on the virtues of *this* person, on his way
of acting in this or that set of circumstances (his *habitus*)
because of who the person is (his or her gender, character,
social status, etc.). Instead, Kant's questions focus on the
agent's will, understood as a disincarnated philosophical
entity, a concept so pure that we can ask whether anything
at all remains.[27] What renders moral the actions of Mr.
Smith, who is a university professor, the father of a family,

25 Ibid., §599.
26 For example, in their proper molecular proportions, hydrogen and
    oxygen are said not to cause water, but to constitute it.
27 For a more precise analysis of this notion, whose plasticity is rightly

a sailor, and a lover of old movies, will be *exactly the same thing* as that which renders moral the acts of Miss Jones, a young, single secretary, living with her parents, and hoping to find the love of her life . . . (to say nothing of Mr. Bakongo, living in a Congolese village, or Mrs. Zhuang, living in a suburb of Shanghai). On the other hand, by appealing to his notion of a "form of life," Wittgenstein shows that the characterization of a person as acting morally presupposes that concepts employed in providing this characterization be understood in light of the use we make of them. These usages are themselves tied to the social practices in which one's psychological and moral vocabularies are embedded. This perspective, however, does not entail radical relativism; or if it does, one would have to say that the *Nicomachean Ethics* and the *Summa theologiae* also encourage moral relativism. The notion that the moral character of an action is entirely external to the description we make of that action seems hardly plausible. Our description will be of a particular person acting in a certain way for a specific reason. In this description, we never have recourse to an interior volitional entity. This is why Wittgenstein's perspective is clearly closer to the conception advanced by Aristotle and Aquinas than to the views maintained by most post-Cartesian philosophers.

Intellect and Will according to St. Thomas

Descartes' intellectual inheritors conceive the will as the faculty of volitions, and volitions as internal events that cause our voluntary actions. Freedom thus consists in having control over these internal events. For Thomas, however, the mind consists of two *powers*, intellect and will. The latter is not a faculty of volitions, but a power we attribute to one who *does* certain things, such as making decisions, just as we attribute intellect to one who understands in a

troubling, see Jean-Pierre Cometti, *Philosopher avec Wittgenstein* (Paris: PUF, 1996).

specifically human way. Even though humans have in common with animals certain appetites that are not uniquely human, the will is the specifically human power of desiring. *The will is the power to have desires that only the intellect can form.* No intellectual capacity is required to desire food or sex; on the other hand, only an intellectual being can desire to worship God or solve a problem of logic, both of which are typically human endeavors.[28]

As post-Kantians, we have difficulty accepting that no sharp distinction exists between the theoretical and practical parts of philosophy, between knowledge and action. Wittgenstein's indifference to this distinction is clear in the importance he accords to the notion that to believe *p* is in the final analysis to *behave* in such a way that we can attribute to you the belief that *p*.[29] This indifference has a key role to play in the dissolution of the internalist tradition in philosophy. It also renders more easily intelligible the link between intellect and will in the Thomistic philosophy of mind.

Like any ancient or medieval philosopher, a modern philosopher will attempt to explain the relationship between reason and desire. He will especially seek to understand how freedom is possible if reason remains the dominant faculty.[30] Yet, the Cartesian solution to this problem, the infinity of the will, is truly original. By refusing what is refused me and by accepting what is given me, I

---

28 Clearly, eroticism or gastronomic refinement are also specifically human realities.

29 This is not a tenet that Wittgenstein explicitly formulates in his works. One can easily see, however, that he often asks himself what difference this or that belief makes *in practice*. This is clear in his reflections concerning mathematics, as François Schmitz has shown in discussing the behavior of *homo mathematicus* (François Schmitz, *Wittgenstein, la philosophie et les mathématiques* [Paris: PUF, 1988]).

30 For more on this interpretation of the metaphysics of the will according to Descartes, see Nicolas Grimaldi, *L'expérience de la pensée dans la philosophie de Descartes* (Paris: Vrin, 1978), 216 and following.

always retain the "free disposition of my volitions."[31] In a very different way, Thomas holds that "by means of universal considerations we can calm our anger or fear, or we can excite them."[32] In the practical syllogism, intellect and will are inextricably linked. The practical syllogism entails "drawing particular conclusions from universal propositions."[33] The will is not the infinite in the creature, but part of intelligence in the rational agent.[34] We cannot emphasize enough the difference between these two philosophical perspectives: for Descartes, practical intellect plays no fundamental role. Only by grasping our moral infinity do we ensure our possession of what Descartes call *generosity*. For Thomas, mastery of our desires belongs to practical rationality. For the moderns, as often is the case for them, morality (or knowledge) is an all-or-nothing endeavor. The ancients and the medievals had a deeper sense of the piecemeal developmental character of morality (and of knowledge). Hence, St. Thomas does not portray the will as the duty that constitutes the sole motive of my actions, which is how Kant portrays it.[35] The command of reason functions in such a way that I want what I *know* to be the best thing to do, given my finality (which pertains to my nature and is nothing other than the happiness of seeing heavenly beatitude) and the circumstances in which I am embedded: my character, my intellectual gifts, and the education I have received.

Some might object that the Thomistic account of human

---

31 René Descartes, *The Passions of the Soul*, §153 (AT 11:446) in *The Philosophical Writings of Descartes*, v. 1, p. 384.
32 *ST* I 81.3: "*applicando enim aliquas universales considerationes, mitigatur ira aut timor aut aliquid huiusmodi, vel etiam instigatur.*"
33 *ST* I 81.3: "*ex universalibus propositionibus concluduntur conclusiones singulares.*"
34 This sentence was revised by the author for the English language edition.
35 Immanuel Kant, *Groundwork of the Metaphysics of Morals*, (Section I), pp. 7–18 (AK 4:393–405).

action is just the sort of disappointingly naïve theory from which modern philosophy has disabused us. There was first Descartes and then Kant. Next, as the product of the nineteenth-century abandonment of metaphysics, there emerged the philosophy of subjectivity, which in turn became psychology, a discipline dedicated to studying the depths of consciousness. In the twentieth century, this became psychoanalysis. Yet the core presupposition remains the same: there exists an interior universe for us to explore. This narrative is itself breezily simplistic. Pitched at the level of a prep-school textbook, no true scholar can take it seriously. It is *precisely* the pedestrian level of the narrative, however, that makes it so powerful, that enables it to retain such a hold on us. Seemingly self-evident, it reveals the part modernity plays in shaping our self-understanding. Since this interior universe is a world of competing forces where no rational mastery is possible, reason's command over the sense appetites thus appears illusory. Henceforth the power of the will can only be contested (Freud and the majority of sociologists), or take the form of an absolute affirmation of subjectivity (Descartes), or even of an absolute affirmation of power for its own sake (Nietzsche). Nonetheless, Thomas – the reading of whom does little to encourage the notion that he is naïve about the human condition – persists in affirming that rational control over our actions is possible. He does so by offering the Aristotelian distinction between despotic and political power.[36] *Despotic power* is exercised over things incapable of resisting it, such as a slave (Aristotle's example) or the body (Aquinas' example). *Political power* is employed on things that retain a certain power of their own, such as a free citizen (Aristotle) or the passions (Aquinas). We can be hindered in the use of our hands or feet, but these members do not themselves will anything. *It is the human agent that*

36 Aristotle, *Politics* b. 1, c. 5 (1254b2).

wills. It is in this sense that "the soul dominates the body by means of a despotic power."[37] We would completely misinterpret Thomas if we were to regard him as affirming disregard for or the repression of the body. Thomas Aquinas does not think in terms of psychological dualism, in terms of two united but ontologically distinct substances, even though the soul for him is not reducible to matter. From this perspective, the soul's command over the body does not imply one force imposing itself on another, as if the body could have volitions of its own. On the other hand, the sense appetites (which are precisely not reducible to the body) have a certain power of their own that can resist the power of reason.[38] The act of the sense appetite occurs under the impetus of the imagination and the senses. The task, therefore, is to establish the diplomatic power of reason: the power of rational appetite over the sense appetites. *The goal is not to abolish our desires, but to have good desires.*

Thomas even affirms that the sense appetite itself, and not just the intellect, can move the will.[39] In saying that the appetite "itself" moves the will, this does not mean that it moves the will as an external mover, but that this appetite is *a certain way of judging* resulting from our dispositions. To be conquered by a desire is still to reason, but to reason *badly.* This moral psychology recognizes the existence of acute cases where all rationality, and *consequently* all will, is absent. This in no way suggests, however, that the existence of such cases invalidates an intellectualist conception of the will. It only reveals that some behavior is not explicable in terms of practical rationality. Thomas concludes, therefore, that "Thus, either there is no movement of the will in the person [as occurs in those who are overcome with rage or in those who are insane, which not all of us

37 *ST* I 81.3 ad 2: *"anima quidem enim corpori dominatur despotico principatu."*
38 On this point, see also *ST* I-II 17.7.
39 *ST* I-II 9.2.

are, or at least not all of the time], and passion alone dominates, or, if there is movement of the will, the person does
not follow passion necessarily."[40]

The opposition between nature and freedom, so integral
to the Kantian analysis of action and thus also to modern
thought, would make little sense to a medieval thinker. We
see this clearly in Thomas' insistence that the act of the will
follows the act of the intellect: "the principles of intellectual knowledge are naturally known."[41] Thomas' naturalism
does not consist in affirming that our will results from
physical or biological nature, but in affirming that it flows
directly from our human nature, in other words, from what
befits us on account of who we are: rational beings, not
beasts or angels.[42] The exercise of the will is thus not something that supervenes in opposition to nature but is the act
itself of our nature. Thomas saw clearly that we can only
understand the will by means of a psychology and an
anthropology that examine not some interior universe, but
human acts. This is what Anscombe, Kenny, and Davidson,
in spite of what divides them, call *the philosophy of mind*. Far
from being some type of foundationalist philosophy, it is a
reflection on our reasons for action, because the will, as the
rational appetite, presupposes that we act *for reasons*. The
will is always the power to act of a rational being as
rational, even though "concerning contingent things, rea-

---

40 *ST* I-II 10.3: "*Et sic aut motus voluntatis non est in homine, sed sola
passio dominatur, aut, si motus voluntatis sit, non ex necessitate sequitur
passionem.*"

41 *ST* I-II 10.1: "*principia intellectualis cognitionis sunt naturaliter nota.*"

42 This is why there is no incompatibility between divine providence,
which creates and directs all things, and human freedom. "Since the
will is an active principle not determined to one thing, but stands
indifferently before many things [because of the act of the intellect
that chooses and of the will that follows it], God moves the will without determining it necessarily to one thing, but lets the will's motion
remain contingent and not necessary, except with respect to those
things toward which it moves naturally" (*ST* I-II 10.4). See also *ST* I
19.8; *ST* I 22.2 and especially *De Malo* 6.

son is able to go in apposite directions, as is clear in dialectical syllogisms and in the suasive arguments proper to rhetoric."[43] It is partly because of this that there is free will(*liberum arbitrium*): the practical syllogism can and should take into account the particular characteristics of the situation, one's dispositions, both natural and acquired (one's character), certain habitual behaviors, and so forth. Citing the *Nicomachean Ethics*,[44] St. Thomas refers to the desiring intellect or the intellectual appetite, underlining the synergistic character of rationality and appetite – the synergistic character that defines the will.[45]

While modern dualism attempts to reduce the question of the passions to that of psychological causality and the ways of bracketing it, St. Thomas distinguishes natural causes from voluntary causes.[46] This is exactly the distinction to which Wittgenstein has accustomed us through his own distinction between an explanation by means of causes and an explanation by means of reasons.[47] With this he helps us grasp Thomas' assertion that the criterion of this distinction is the will itself. An animal can have habits (one can train a dog by hitting it with a stick), but a mere animal never acquires a *habitus* (disposition). A *habitus* is something one exercises *when one wants* to exercise it. The reason for my action, which is not its cause, is the intention at work in this action. "Intention of an end implies the ordering of something to that end, which pertains to reason."[48] Brute animals lack this ability. Although the distinction between *causes* and *reasons* has been disputed by Davidson

---

43 *ST* I 83.1: "*Ratio enim circa contingentia habet viam ad opposita; ut patet in dialecticis syllogismis, et rhetoricis persuasionibus.*"
44 Aristotle, *Nicomachean Ethics*, b. 3, c. 3 (1113a11) and b. 6, c. 2 (1139b4).
45 *ST* I 83.3.
46 *ST* I-II 50.3.
47 Ludwig Wittgenstein, *Blue and Brown Books* (Oxford: Blackwell, 1964), 14–15. See the analysis offered by Ruwen Ogien, *Les causes et les raisons* (Nîmes: Éd. J. Chambon, 1995), 36–39.
48 *ST* I-II 12.5 *sed contra*: "*intentio finis importat ordinationem alicuius in finem quod est rationis.*"

and others, this is not the important point to recognize. Rather, from the perspective of our inquiry's focus, *St. Thomas considered as a post-Wittgensteinian*, the point is that a distinction at the center of discussions in the analytic philosophy of mind and of action, and taken up by Wittgenstein, was already explicitly present in the works of Thomas Aquinas.

What makes the voluntary character of an act properly human is that "the principle of certain acts or movements is in the agent."[49] We should not, however, interpret this as a post-Cartesian would. We should not see it as implying that the will functions as an inner agent acting from within an ephemeral interior world.[50] What is important for Thomas is knowledge of the end. Only someone who knows the end possesses the principle of his own actions. In other words, only one who acts from reasons that he knows can be said to will. This means simply that he would be able to give his reasons if they were demanded of him. It does not mean that his actions presuppose first a self-reflective moment, a sort of initial colloquy with oneself. Nor does voluntary action presuppose the absolute priority of a principle of action, as Kantians hold when they refuse to consider as authentically voluntary any principle of action preceded by sense inclinations, social habits, or divine determination (which, however, is unavoidable if God is the first mover, as he is for St. Thomas). As Thomas explains, "it is not essential to the notion of the voluntary that its intrinsic principle be the first principle."[51] Setting aside the issue of the divine will, what matters is that the rational agent knows the sense inclinations for what they are. On the level of voluntary movement, although the principle is not the first, it is the one that makes the act

---

49 *ST* I-II 6.1: "*quorundam actuum seu motuum principium est in agente.*"
50 This sentence was revised by the author for the English language edition.
51 *ST* I-II 6.1 ad 1: "*non est de ratione voluntarii quod principium intrinsecum sit principium primum.*"

occur. This is what matters. It is not as if, on the level of the sense appetites, inclinations play no part in forming our reasons for action. In other words, absolute moral spontaneity is not a necessary component of this characterization of the voluntary: the will acts as the appetitive component of a practical understanding of constraints and not as the eradication of all external causes for the sake of a pure practical reason.

From the many possible examples, let us take one from the part of the *Summa theologiae* dedicated to human acts. The third objection from ST I-II 7.3 almost seems like it could have been written by Kant himself: "circumstances are not of the substance of an act; the causes of an act belong to the substance of the act."[52] Let us translate this into Kantian language: the circumstances of an act constitute the empirical conditions of its realization and are thus exterior. The moral act, for Kant, can only be governed by a categorical (and not a hypothetical) imperative. The good will is not a principle of action governed by the intellect in its act of conforming what is done to the circumstances of the act. If one follows Thomas, however, the Kantian hypothesis rests on a false conception of what an *act* is.[53] This is so because, "something is called a circumstance because, although it exists outside the substance of the act, it touches it in some way."[54] In fact, "when studying acts, we should consider who did it, by what means or instruments he did it, what he did, where he did it, why he did it, and how and when he did it."[55] Hence, although "being good or evil is not a circumstance, it results from all the cir-

---

52 *ST* I-II 7.3 obj. 3: *"circumstantiae non sunt de substantia actus. sed ad substantiam actus pertinere videntur causae ipsius actus."*

53 In general, for a Thomist the weakness of the Kantian analysis of morality is due to the weakness of its moral psychology, or even of its anthropology, as I have suggested elsewhere (Roger Pouivet, *Esthétique et logique* [Liège: Mardaga, 1996], 48).

54 *ST* I-II 7.3: *"circumstantia dicitur quod, extra substantiam actus existens, aliquo modo attingit ipsum."*

55 *ST* I-II 7.3: *"Considerandum est enim in actibus quis fecit, quibus auxiliis*

cumstances."[56] This fact reinforces the notion that a voluntary act has an intellectual character. The will becomes viewed as the appetitive component of an active understanding of ends, and more particularly of an end that orders all the others, all the while taking into account what is done, what is actually brought about, since the end does not justify every means, every resulting act.[57] What matters is that the end be a real and not an apparent good.[58] Once again we see the importance of the intellect. Even though the human person is naturally drawn toward the good, he is not drawn to it independently of his intellectual capacity, and this is why he can be wrong (and why, for St. Thomas, he can sin). Thus, when Thomas affirms that the will can move itself,[59] he is not asserting the moral sovereignty of the will as a pure moral principle, but only the understanding of the end that is the object of willing. This to such an extent that we can even say that the will is moved by an exterior principle.[60] If I wish to regain my health, I deliberate about the means to obtaining health. Yet, if I wish to regain my health, this is *because* I am sick. This is what pushes me to will. Nevertheless, the will is only moved by itself. It is simply that this self-movement must begin *for a reason* that is an exterior principle (in this case a sickness that is not willed). This is why "even though the proximate principle of voluntary movement is intrinsic, its first principle is exterior."[61]

The heart of St. Thomas' theory of the will is the defini-

---

vel instrumentis fecerit, quid fecerit, ubi fecerit, cur fecerit, quomodo fecerit, et quando fecerit."

56 *ST* I-II 7.3 ad 2: *"iste modus qui est bene vel male, non ponitur circumstantia, sed consequens ad omnes circumstantias."*

57 This sentence and the final sentence of the previous paragraph were revised by the author for the English language edition.

58 *ST* I-II 8.1.

59 *ST* I-II 9.3.

60 *ST* I-II 9.4.

61 *ST* I-II 9.4 ad 1: *"motus voluntarius etsi habeat principium proximum intrinsecum, tamen principium primum est ab extra."*

tion of choice as desiderative intellect or intellectual desire.[62] Thomas states that "the act by which the will tends to something proposed to it as good, from the fact that it is ordered to the end by reason, is materially from the will but formally from reason."[63] Choice, therefore, is not merely a simple consequence of judgment, but is the judgment itself as executory: "the conclusion itself seems to belong to the choice as its consequence."[64] Choice presupposes the effective capacity of judgment that involves the will. This is why brute animals, since their behavior is only determined by the sense appetite, cannot make choices.[65] We would never describe the actions of someone known to lack the ability to make rational judgments as a *choice*. An action can be called intentional only if it can also be described as the act of one who knows the end of his action. That we can also describe the act as chosen stems from the fact that the practical syllogism concerns the means to the end. Choice, therefore, is not an indefinite openness to all possibilities or a freedom of indifference (a choice between contraries). It is a decision concerning what we should do to attain the end, and this in light of what is *possible* for us to do.[66] Thomas even affirms that "the means to the end, which is what choice is about, relate to the end the way a conclusion

---

62 *ST* I-II 13.1: "*electio est appetitivus intellectus, vel appetitus intellectivus.*"
63 *ST* I-II 13.1: "*ille actus quo voluntas tendit in aliquid quod proponitur ut bonum, ex eo quod per rationem est ordinatum ad finem, materialiter quidem est voluntatis, formaliter autem rationis.*"
64 *ST* I-II 13.1 ad 2: "*ipsa conclusio pertinere videtur ad electionem, tanquam ad consequens.*"
65 *ST* I-II 13.2.
66 *ST* I-II 13.5. To describe a person as wishful, as engaging in wishful thinking, implies that he wants the impossible as if it were possible. Choice, however, is not about the impossible. There is therefore in wishful behavior a lack of practical judgment, whereby what is impossible is allowed to enter into one's decisions. While it does sometimes happen that we choose things that are impossible, the wishful person is one who lives from the intellectual vice of allowing impossibilities into his judgments. We should note the *modal* component of practical judgment, which renders it a very complicated judgment from the perspective of logic – as the studies of Georg

relates to its principle."[67] Thus, we can say that "the will is intermediate between intellect and exterior operation."[68] Practical reasoning establishes what we should do in light of the end or of the intermediate ends. In the language of contemporary logic, we can say that practical reasoning is not a monotone.[69] In other words, one cannot add a premise to a collection of premises without checking to see whether the conclusion still follows from such premises. Hence, although practical reasoning is truly *reasoning*, it is not so conclusive that willing an end necessarily leads to the choice of a means. It always remains possible for a supervening premise to call into question the conclusion, in other words, the choice.

Free Decision (Liberum Arbitrium) and an Ephemeral Freedom

To say that practical reasoning is non-monotone (reversible) is to recognize that "there is great uncertainty in discerning what should be done, because actions are about contingent singulars, which because of their variability are uncertain."[70] This is why there is deliberation. Deliberation is a type of inquiry about what is to be done.

Henrik Von Wright have shown. On practical rationality in general, see *Practical Reasoning*, edited by Joseph Raz (Oxford: Oxford University Press, 1978).

67 *ST* I-II 13.5: "*Sic enim se habet id quod est ad finem, de quo electio est, ad finem, sicut conclusio ad principium.*"

68 *ST* I-II 13.5 ad 1: "*voluntas media est inter intellectum et exteriorem operationem.*"

69 Thomas clearly did not employ this notion of monotonality, but he seems to have something like this in mind when he affirms that "a conclusion does not always follow necessarily from its principles, but only in the case where the principles cannot be true if the conclusion is not true" (*ST* I-II 13.6 ad 1). If practical reasoning is inductive, then clearly the conclusion can be false even when the principles are true. Concerning non-monotone reasoning, see Eric Grégoire, *Logique non monotones et intelligence artificielle* (Paris: Hermès, 1990).

70 *ST* I-II 14.1: "*In rebus autem agendis multa incertitudo invenitur, quia actiones sunt circa singularia contingentia, quae propter sui variabilitatem incerta sunt.*"

It is an inquiry subject to all the hazards of the agent's personal endowments and the circumstances in which he or she acts. It is an analytic inquiry because it begins with the end as its principle and moves toward a consideration of the means toward that end – this is why the order of reasoning about our acts is the inverse of the order proper to the action itself. We should note that for Thomas, *when I deliberate the ball is already in play*. Deliberation is not about the end, but about the means, about what is contingent. The notion that freedom could imply such a complete indeterminism that deliberation wouldn't incline toward anything – a notion that is widespread among modern philosophers – is simply absurd. Deliberation is undertaken in order to determine what we should do, not in order to reassure ourselves constantly that we could have acted other than we did without having any reason to do so. The outcome of deliberation, therefore, is not the acceptance or rejection of determinism, but consent. This is what marks the difference between undergoing a change (which is what happens to the brute animals) and acting.[71]

Yet, isn't the Thomistic analysis of the will's commanded acts (of acts "that are commanded by the will by means of the motive power")[72] clearly infected by privatism?[73] There is, of course, no hint of privatism – of a secondary act flowing from the interiority of the will – in Aquinas' account of the will's immediate acts (to enjoy, choose, deliberate, consent). To will is to enjoy, to choose, to deliberate, and to consent. The will is actualized in certain human dispositions. The term *actus* (reality) in *actus voluntatis* (the reality of the will) does not designate an inte-

---

71 *ST* I-II 15.2.
72 *ST* I-II 6.4: "[actus] qui a voluntate imperantur mediante potentia motiva."
73 As the author explains in chapter three, "privatism maintains that the psychological concepts proper to humans acquire their meaning in relation to an interior event internal to the mind." At issue here is whether concepts necessarily acquire their *meaning* through a cognitive act of interior reflection upon them. –*Trans.*

rior event, but the exercise of the will itself. Instead of being some disembodied inner event, this act constitutes the way beings endowed with intellect and appetite behave.[74] The voluntary act actualizes a faculty and not a mental event. The will's act is not a volitional pre-act that is subsequently followed by the act willed. Nevertheless, isn't this how Aquinas describes acts *commanded* by the will, acts that don't proceed directly from the will? Isn't privatism lurking there?

St. Thomas draws on a quotation from Aristotle to offer a key precision: "'where one thing exists on account of another, there is really only one thing' (*Topics* b. 3, c. 2 [117a18]). But the commanded act only exists on account of command. Therefore, command and the act commanded are one."[75] The voluntary act in itself is absolutely one, but multiple from the vantage point of philosophical analysis. Consequently, although we can recognize the existence of a command that makes the act voluntary, this does not mean that there is a private mental event that causes and is really distinct from the voluntary act. Thomas readily grants that "in things multiple according to their parts but one according to the whole, nothing prevents there being a priority of one thing over another, as, for example, the soul has a certain priority over the body, and the heart has a certain priority over the other members."[76] Hence, one can of course portray command as what causes the voluntary act. Nevertheless, this does not mean that volition is something separate, an interior act of the will. Such an act would presuppose beforehand another volitional act possessing an even deeper interiority, implying an infinite regression that

---

74 This sentence was revised by the author for the English-language edition.

75 *ST* I-II 17.4 *sed contra*: "'ubi est unum propter alterum, ibi est unum tantum.' sed actus imperatus non est nisi propter imperium. ergo sunt unum."

76 *ST* I-II 17.4 ad 3: "nihil prohibet in his quae sunt multa partibus et unum toto, unum esse prius alio. Sicut anima quodammodo est prius corpore, et cor est prius aliis membris."

would never plumb the hidden recesses of the soul.

The affirmation, "if I go outside it is because I want to go outside," in no way commits me to affirming the existence of a prior act: willing to go outside. I simply look out the window, see that it is a beautiful day, save my work onto a diskette (prudence), stand up, put on my shoes, look for my sunglasses, and then I go out and take a walk. This is what *to will to go outside* means. If someone were to ask me *why* I am outside, I would refer to the beauty of the afternoon and say, I wanted to go outside. If one were then to ask me, "but did you will to will this?" this would seem bizarre to me. If one were further to ask, how long did the willing to go outside last before the going outside began, such a question would clearly seem deranged. Kenny rightly remarks that, "the metaphor of the will issuing commands is an appropriate one, and the comparison between the relationship of command to execution and the relationship of willing to acting is a fruitful one."[77] One must be careful, however, not to be led astray by the metaphor. The metaphor is welcome because it helps us see the analogy between a command given by one who has authority ("do p") and the will (to will p). It is worthy of note that in both cases p is stated. To will p is not a concealed interior event, but the ordering of the series of our acts such that if one were to ask me what I am doing, I could describe the whole series as to will p. Borrowing from Wittgenstein, we can say that nothing is concealed.[78] That I know better than anyone else what I will is not tied to the interiority of my volitions, but to the preferred status habitually accorded to descriptions we *ourselves* make of the series of our acts. The privilege of the first-person per-

77 Anthony Kenny, *Aquinas on Mind* (London: Routledge, 1993), 87.

78 Ludwig Wittgenstein, *Philosophical Investigations*, I §435; the context of Wittgenstein's comment is, of course, somewhat different. He is referring to the representative characters of phrases. Yet, extrapolating his remark to the context of the will seems justified because of the entire analysis that precedes this remark.

spective is one of authority in the correct description of one's acts and not one of privileged access to the contents of consciousness.

CHAPTER SIX
A PHILOSOPHICAL TRADITION

The proposal offered in this book has been to read St. Thomas as a successor of Wittgenstein. Yet, isn't this to abuse both philosophers, or worse, to misinterpret completely their respective positions? This objection is weighty enough to deserve attention even within the limits of this slender volume.

Thomisms

The first chapter of this book contains a chronological sketch of Thomism, or better, of Thomisms. If one accepts the notion that one criterion for being counted among the "great authors" is precisely the multiplicity of *acceptable* interpretations of that author's work, and thus the philosophical fruitfulness of reading his or her work, then we shouldn't be surprised by the plurality of Thomisms, nor by the Thomism proposed here.

St. Thomas fashioned a difficult synthesis of Augustinianism and Arab Aristotelianism. In the years that followed, this synthesis was constantly challenged. In many ways the history of medieval philosophy after Thomas is the history of the dismemberment of the Thomistic synthesis. Modern philosophy will, in a manner of speaking, ignore St. Thomas, or it will present him – with the miraculous exception of Leibniz – as a caricature of Aristotle, disfigured by having all the defects of religious authoritarianism affixed to him. As an indirect consequence of this, the renaissance Thomism of the nineteenth and early twentieth centuries will principally be anti-modern. The reading of Aquinas offered in this book in no way lays claim to this anti-modern heritage. The philosophy of Wittgenstein reveals that there was no need to have despaired of modernity to such a degree: fundamental tenets of Thomism found new expression in the work of an Austrian philosopher living in Cambridge.

But this reading of Aquinas is also not part of a larger effort to promote medieval philosophy in the universities. Such a procedure has fostered, and perhaps will continue to foster, two unfortunate results. It has caused medieval philosophy either to be unjustly held in disrepute by the proponents of ancient and modern philosophy, or to become contaminated by the exegetical and semantic concerns that arose principally in later analytic philosophy (in other words, after Frege, Wittgenstein, and Russell). This second result constitutes a betrayal of Aquinas' texts, which now seem to require reassessment in light of a plethora of medieval Christian, Muslim, and Jewish authors who considered the same questions he did. It goes without saying that erudition should be sought when lacking and praised when present. The avenues for philosophical reflection it opens are indeed respectable. This technical erudition, however, has the disadvantage of consigning St. Thomas, and medieval philosophy generally, into a sort of medievalist ghetto. Let us suppose we were told that a reading of Plato requires that we know who the participants in the dialogues are, whether this or that thesis was actually held by a given interlocutor somewhere else in a specific text of his, and whether certain notions were expressed in writing by someone else a few years before Plato composed a given dialogue. Here again, all of this is certainly an indispensable part of any serious historical and exegetical work. Yet, the moment one wants to offer an interpretation that is not strictly historiographic or exegetical, no matter what one claims, one ends up in reality doing something else. For example, one ends up, as Alain de Libéra does, "inscribing the history of universals into a larger history in order to assess how this problematic reoccurs, beyond the discontinuity of *epistemai*, as one single and self-same history,"[1] even asserting that "the history of universals is a history of the *logos*."[2] In other words, one winds up taking from Foucault principles of interpretation carefully attuned to Heideggerian perspectives on the history of philosophy. In short, in spite of everything, it is from today and *looking backwards* that one reads the medievals. Could one ever do otherwise, even if one were more or less to accentuate the historical tenor of one's reflections?

From this we can conclude that when one interprets Thomas Aquinas, it is *always* contemporary philosophers that one is confronting.[3] What I have presented here, through my synthesis of the works of Anscombe, Geach, Kenny, and MacIntyre, has a certain particularity, especial-

1 Alain de Libéra, *La querelle des universaux de Platon à la fin du Moyen Age* (Paris: Éd. du Seuil, 1996), 451.

2 Alain de Libéra, *La querelle des universaux*, 452.

3 As John Marenbon has noted, at issue is the very conception of what philosophy should be. See John Marenbon, *Later Medieval Philosophy* (London: Routledge and Kegan Paul, 1987), 88. The theory that one can understand a philosopher the way he understood himself presupposes that meanings are accessible to us the same way they were accessible to the author himself. This thesis seems to be a form of Platonism or of Structuralism (which in this instance amounts to the same thing) peculiar to the history of philosophy. Once again, to reject this conception is not to authorize an *anything-goes* attitude in the history of philosophy or in any other domain. The assertion that attempting to reconstruct the true thought of an author is a fundamentally wrongly defined project does not change the fact that ignorance and anachronism are vices opposed to virtue. Without being able to develop it here, we would say that in the history of philosophy, although nothing is certain, this does not mean that everything is possible.

ly in comparison with the above-cited perspective articulated by Foucault and Heidegger. By affirming that a large portion of Aquinas' work is true and by attempting to defend what rightly could be true in it, my work is itself *Thomist*. By true here I mean something very simple: that which corresponds to things as they are. The general perspective advanced by modern philosophy – with its emphasis upon *the question of the subject* – faces evident difficulties, as, for example, its view that the contents of consciousness are reflexively accessible as the ground of knowledge.[4] In this domain, what reveals the *truth* of Thomas Aquinas' philosophy of mind is its basic point of departure. It does not attempt to analyze the contents of the consciousness of a *subject* of knowledge and action. Instead, it analyzes human knowledge and human acts. The problem of knowledge is not the problem of its foundations and the conditions for its possibility (idealism), but the problem of understanding *what is known*, because the existence of knowledge, as a fact of human nature, is not in doubt (realism). In the philosophy of mind, the issue of the will always reduces to the challenge of explaining how a unique type of reasoning functions, a type of reasoning in which the conclusion is not merely a reason for acting, but an act itself.

The notion that a Thomist philosophy can develop out of a reading of Wittgenstein nevertheless seems vulnerable to the objection that for St. Thomas philosophy – even the philosophy of mind – was the "maidservant of theology" (*ancilla theologiae*). As Alain de Libéra affirms, "one cannot understand the significance of the Thomistic perspective until one sees that it adheres to the Aristotelian epistemology for reasons that are both philosophical and *theological*."[5] Without doubt the same could be said of anything Thomas

---

4 This sentence was revised by the author for the English-language edition.

5 Alain de Libéra, *La querelle des universaux*, 262.

affirms. Indeed, it could be said of anything any committed Christian affirms. For, if you take seriously the notion that the world is created, if you hold this *literally*, then it is difficult to see what could fall outside a theological *summa*. This, however, does not prevent us from detaching Thomas' philosophy of mind from his theology. Indeed, certain medieval theologians did *not* adhere to the Aristotelian epistemology *precisely* for reasons that were both philosophical and *theological*. St. Thomas' theology, therefore, is not the necessary or even sufficient reason for his adopting Aristotelianism. When Thomas asks what it means to think and to will, his answer is no doubt compatible with his theology, but it is in no way dictated by it. In other words, it is separable from it.[6] Clearly, even if one were to cut away St. Thomas' theology from his philosophy, one would still not arrive at a secular form of philosophy. Nevertheless, even among philosophers, the number of philosophers for whom God plays a major role is not negligible.

Throughout its history, philosophy is almost always linked to other preoccupations, be they scientific, religious, historical, poetic, political, or polemic. This, however, does not prevent us from considering the philosophical theses of this or that author independently of these particular concerns. We can read Plato's *Dialogues* as works of philosophy while detaching them from Plato's political preoccupations. We can read Descartes' *Discourse on Method* as a reflection on certitude, and not merely as a preface to his

6   The "separationist" perspective, according to which we can *separate* Thomas' philosophy from his theology, affirming that St. Thomas himself makes this distinction, is defended by Fernand Van Steenberghen, as is clear from his study, *Le thomisme*, the "Que saisje" series (Paris: PUF, 1983). See also his other works that treat St. Thomas. Etienne Gilson held that philosophy could be separated from theology, but in his discussions of *Christian philosophy* (a philosophy completely transformed by the advent of Christ), Gilson's reconstruction of St. Thomas' philosophy is larger than strict separationists would allow.

(partially obsolete) scientific treatises. We can read Arnauld's letters to Leibniz as a metaphysics of modalities, without embracing the view that his metaphysics only makes sense from within a particular religious perspective. If we still read the philosophers of the past, this is precisely because what they say still interests us, even though they said these things from within a framework that was not strictly philosophical, if there is such a thing as a strictly philosophical framework. What they say interests us because what they say could be true.[7] Thomas Aquinas' philosophy of mind would be "the right one," independently of his religious preoccupations, or, as some would say, in spite of them. This, at least, appears to be the view of Anscombe, Kenny, and MacIntyre.

St. Thomas himself said that, in discussions with *pagans* "we must have recourse to natural reason, to which all people assent," even though "concerning divine realities it is deficient."[8] Philosophy and theology do not stand in mutual isolation. Yet, the arguments of one can often be distinguished and detached from the arguments of the other. However this may be, and without entering more deeply into the methodological debates surrounding the study of medieval thinkers, there is no doubt that analytic philoso-

7   As Claude Panaccio remarks, to take a philosopher seriously presupposes that we enter "the game of alethetic evaluation" (Claude Panaccio, *Les mots, les concepts et les choses* [Paris: Vrin, 1991], 17). To suspend the question of knowing whether what a philosopher says is true or false, if it is even possible to understand what he is saying without posing the question of its truth or falsity, is to treat philosophies as cultural artifacts or as objects of merely esthetical worth. For a defense of the idea of truth in the history of philosophy see also Jean-Marie Beyssade, *La philosophie première de Descartes* (Paris: Flammarion, 1979), vi.

8   *Summa Contra Gentiles* I c. 2, n. 4: "*unde necesse est ad naturalem rationem recurrere, cui omnes assentire coguntur. quae tamen in rebus divinis deficiens est.*" As directed toward a non-Christian audience, the perspective of this *Summa* is clearly favorable to the idea of detaching philosophy from theology, a perspective less in evidence in the *Summa theologiae*.

phers such as Anscombe, Geach, and Kenny think that Thomas' philosophy can be detached from his theology.[9] As Kenny suggests, although Thomas as a theologian proposes a rational defense of the dogmas of the Christian faith as presented in the sacred scriptures and the teachings of the Church: "as a philosopher, his task is to get as far as he can in discovering what kind of place the world is, and what truths we can know which are necessary truths about the world and about ourselves, discoverable by unaided reason, without appealing to any alleged divine revelation."[10]

In What Sense Is Wittgenstein a Philosopher?

An even more serious objection comes from asking how one can seriously consider Wittgenstein to belong to the same philosophical *tradition* as St. Thomas, one of the theologians of the Church? Indeed, since Thomas begins with *the (revealed) truth*, which he is not seeking to find but only to defend rationally, he has often been regarded as one of the most dogmatic of thinkers. This objection rests on the meaning one gives to "tradition." In the history of philosophy, traditions are not something we discover pre-made, but are something we ourselves fashion. For example, Deleuze proposed a philosophical tradition consisting of Lucretius, Spinoza, Hume, Nietzsche, and Bergson. Without Deleuze, who would ever have thought of placing these thinkers together? Indeed, doubts remain concerning the relevance of such an assemblage. On the other hand, the view that an intellectual continuity exists between scholastic and analytic philosophy seems clear to many,

---

9   Claude Panaccio also defends this thesis concerning William of Ockham (see Claude Panaccio, *Les mots, les concepts et les choses*, 21). He defends his conception of the history of philosophy in "De la reconstruction en histoire de la philosophie," in *La philosophie et son histoire: essais et discussions*, edited by Gilbert Boss (Zurich: Éd. du Grand Midi, 1994), 173–95.

10 Anthony Kenny, *Aquinas on Mind* (London: Routledge, 1993), 12.

even if they often concentrate on the most technical conti-
nuities concerning logic, linguistic analysis, and the semantics of modalities.[11] Hence, to affirm that the philosophy of
mind of contemporary authors such as Anscombe, Geach,
and Kenny stands in continuity with the philosophies of
Aristotle and Aquinas is to define an Aristotelian tradition
to which belong philosophers who have not been touched
by Cartesian modernism. For them, *reflexive* philosophy, as
a philosophy of interiority, is simply an enormous error.[12]
Our hope is that this book has at least rendered plausible
the hypothesis that such an Aristotelian tradition exists,
one in which St. Thomas and Wittgenstein play crucial
roles.

One could of course object that Wittgenstein is not a
philosopher amenable to being attached to a tradition
because instead of seeking solutions to philosophical problems, he strove instead to show that in most cases such
problems don't even exist, being the result of the typical
ways philosophers empty language of meaning.[13]

11 This is the fundamental hypothesis of the promoters of the monu-
mental *Cambridge History of Later Medieval Philosophy,* edited by
Norman Kretzman, Anthony Kenny, Jan Pinborg, and Eleonore
Stump (Cambridge: Cambridge University Press, 1982) as well as the
majority of the current Anglo-American specialists in medieval philosophy. This perspective is not reserved merely for the philosophers
of the fourteenth century, which would seem more natural. It can
also be extended to Thomas, as we suggest in this book, or to St.
Anselm, as David K. Lewis does in "Anselm and Actuality," in
Philosophical Papers (Oxford: Oxford University Press, 1983), vol. 1,
pp. 10–25. For two other studies that advance a similar argument, see
Peter Geach, *Reference and Generality, an Examination of Some Medieval
and Modern Theories* (Ithaca, N.Y.: Cornell University Press, 1962) and
Alexander Broadie, *Introduction to Medieval Logic* (Oxford: Clarendon
Press, 1993). For a discussion of this annexation of medieval philosophy by analytic philosophy, see also Alasdair MacIntyre's critique
in *Three Rival Versions of Moral Enquiry* (Notre Dame, Ind.: University
of Notre Dame Press, 1990), 160–62.

12 There are other core features of this tradition that we might consider, such as that it takes seriously the problem of natural species.

13 This problem is clearly raised by Jean-Pierre Cometti, *Philosopher avec*

Attempting to call Wittgenstein an Aristotelian makes as much sense as calling him a *positivist*, which is how he was often described in the 1930s (and sometimes still is described today in France). We could perhaps respond to this objection by saying that not *all* philosophers empty language of meaning – and the members of the Aristotelian tradition much less so. Yet, this response would not satisfy the objector.

Our fuller response, therefore, is that the current in analytic philosophy to which this book belongs rejects the view that Wittgenstein's thought is somehow *without precedent*. Some interpreters of Wittgenstein regard features of his thought as impossible to assimilate into their philosophical tradition, a tradition that emphasizes linguistic analysis and argument (the analytical tradition). To be frank, we view these features of Wittgenstein as merely problems of style. To the extent that it is possible in philosophy, as elsewhere, to separate style from content – not, indeed, entirely, but at least somewhat and sometimes significantly – it is not the content of what Wittgenstein says, but his way of saying it that is without common measure. Wittgenstein's hostility toward metaphysics is also found in Kant. His rejection of essentialist theories of knowledge is present among many fourteenth-century scholastics. His naturalist anthropology is already present in Hume, and his dispositionalism in Aristotle. Indeed, even the idea of philosophy as therapeutic is not new.[14] One could of course say that Wittgenstein doesn't advance a single thesis, that he doesn't even really do philosophy, but encourages us to stop doing it. Yet, doesn't he critique metaphysics? Doesn't

Wittgenstein (Paris: PUF, 1996). Wittgenstein could well have raised such an objection himself.

14 Besides belonging to a venerable tradition in Antiquity, one finds it with Descartes himself, as Mike Marlies shows in "Doubt, Reason and Cartesian Therapy," in *Descartes, Critical and Interpretive Essays*, edited by Michael Hooker (Baltimore: Johns Hopkins University Press, 1973), 89–113.

he reject essentialism? Isn't his anthropology naturalist? And what is all of this, if not philosophy, now as always?

Is the difference between traditional philosophy and the thought of Wittgenstein really so great as he himself seemed to think, as some of his interpreters think, and above all as some of his detractors think?[15] Wittgenstein is a *far more traditional* philosopher than those who affirm that all philosophy after Plato was wrong concerning the fundamental question of subjectivity (an interpretation stemming from Descartes and renewed by Husserl), or than those who attempt to rewrite the entire history of metaphysics as forgetfulness (Heidegger), or even than those who reduce all philosophy to expressions of power or forms of resentment (a current stemming from Nietzsche and developed by Deleuze and Derrida). Who is more concerned with the classical problems of philosophy (the accessibility of the contents of thought, the meaning of affirmations, etc.): Wittgenstein or the above-mentioned philosophers? His philosophic style is without doubt original. The interpretation offered in this book does perhaps minimize the peculiarities of this style and underplay certain existentialist and Kierkegaardian aspects of Wittgenstein. Nevertheless, it seems to us that our interpretation retains its interest.

To say that Descartes' philosophy constitutes a decisive rupture in the history of ideas is not an original view. To insist that this rupture was a *negative* event, could lead one to conclude that we are proposing a neo-neo-scholasticism. Yet, to say that after Wittgenstein the internalist parenthesis has been closed, this is more novel. Far from being an anti-philosopher, Wittgenstein reconciles us with the philosophical tradition that has Thomas Aquinas, in line with Aristotle, as its angelic doctor.

15 See Anthony Kenny, *The Legacy of Wittgenstein* (Oxford: Blackwell, 1984), 57–60.

APPENDIX
How to Understand the Notion of a Phantasm[1]
(St. Thomas and Quine)

Bernard Lonergan affirms that "Human intellect in this life needs phantasms as objects – indeed, as proper objects. Since knowledge requires an object, and since phantasm is the object of intellect, a phantasm is always necessary for intellectual activity, no matter how perfect the *species intelligibilis* [intelligible species]."[2] Sometimes the phantasm produces the act to be understood. This is exactly what happens when a given example enables one to understand (a color sample, example of a courageous act, etc.). As Lonergan notes, this presupposes as well that "informed intellect guides the production of an appropriate phantasm."[3] To understand, doesn't this consist in being able to find good examples, to provoke relevant phantasms?[4]

1 This appendix is meant to complete the analysis of "intentionality" offered in chapter four.
2 Bernard Lonergan, "The Concept of *Verbum* in the Writings of St. Thomas Aquinas" *Theological Studies* 7 (1946): 375.
3 Ibid., 376.
4 The function of an example, therefore, differs entirely from the function of an illustration. The use of a concept is linked to asking for an example in order to know whether we have understood, or to the giving of an example to show that we have understood. Comprehension occurs with the exemplification and can never be entirely detached from it. This of course reminds us of Wittgenstein in his later period.

Etienne Gilson states that the phantasm "is the image of a particular thing: *similitudo rei particularis* [ST I 84.7 ad 2]."[5] The objects cause sense species, which, being similar to the objects, act upon the proper senses, sight, hearing, taste, and then upon the common sense.[6] This operation seems very *material*. So much so, we could even employ contemporary language and describe the sense species as the *stimuli*.[7] Norman Kretzmann states that "phantasms are likenesses of particular material things re-realized in physical configurations of the organ of phantasia, which Aquinas located in the brain."[8] Although Kretzmann does not employ the term *stimulus*, what he says about the phantasms suggests that this is what he means. It is this (daring?) interpretation of the Thomistic conception of the phantasm that I shall offer here.

In the *Pursuit of Truth*, Quine states that "From impacts on our sensory surfaces [from *stimuli*], we in our collective and cumulative creativity down the generations have projected our systematic theory of the external world."[9] Understanding what these impacts are belongs to the

---

5   Etienne Gilson, *The Christian Philosophy of St. Thomas Aquinas*, translated by L. K. Shook (New York: Random House, 1956), 217.

6   See *ST* I 78.3–4.

7   See Etienne Gilson, *The Christian Philosophy of St. Thomas Aquinas*, p. 473, n. 32.

8   Norman Kretzmann, "Philosophy of Mind," in *Cambridge Companion to Aquinas*, edited by Norman Kretzmann and Eleonore Stump (Cambridge: Cambridge University Press, 1993), 140.

9   W. V. Quine, *Pursuit of Truth* (Cambridge, Mass.: Harvard University Press, 1990), 1. The type of evolutionism embraced by Quine is incompatible with the Thomistic understanding of creation. Yet, with respect to the questions that concern us here, this aspect of Quine's thought does not play a significant role. For a non-evolutionist perspective from within the contemporary philosophy of knowledge, inspired in one way by St. Thomas (but above all by Thomas Reid), see Alvin Plantinga, *Warrant and Proper Function* (Oxford: Oxford University Press, 1993), especially chapters 1, 2, 11, and 12. (Plantinga's critique of internalism was already noted in our first chapter.) See also William P. Alston, *The Reliability of Sense Perception* (Ithaca, N.Y.: Cornell University Press, 1993).

neurosciences; it is not an issue for philosophy. It is not surprising, therefore, that Aquinas is no more articulate than Quine when it comes to something about which philosophy can say little.[10] Quine clarifies that what the philosopher can say is that statements of fact are,

> directly and firmly associated with our stimulations. Each should be associated affirmatively with some range of one's stimulations and negatively with some range. The sentence should command the subject's assent or dissent outright, on the occasion of a stimulation in the appropriate range, without further investigation and independently of what he may have been engaged in at the time. A further requirement is intersubjectivity: unlike a report of a feeling, the sentence must command the same verdict from all linguistically competent witnesses of the occasion.[11]

These are sentences such as "it rains," "it is cold," "see the rabbit."

The theory of intelligible and sense species developed by Aquinas and reconstructed with the aid of Quine[12] would thus have the following general structure.

a) Knowledge of a thing, or that a thing is this or that, presupposes identity between knower and known.

b) This identity signifies that what exists *in esse naturale* in the thing and what exists *in esse intentionale* in the mind are the same thing.[13]

---

10 One could object that the division of tasks between science and philosophy was not recognized by St. Thomas, and that it is a modern notion. Yet, it seems that Quine belongs to those philosophers for whom philosophy, at least as they practice it, belongs to the domain of science, being given the task of only asking questions of the most general sort (as Quine says, for example, in *Theories and Things* [Cambridge, Mass.: Harvard University Press, 1981], 191).

11 W. V. Quine, *Pursuit of Truth*, 3.

12 Our final chapter above considers the relevance of this method.

13 For the meaning of these terms, see the glossary.

c) The human intellect knows by means of intelligible species (concepts) whose meaning comes from how they are used (and not from ideal entities).

d) This usage manifests itself in our (intellectual) capacities, such as classifying, distinguishing, and attributing properties.

e) These classifications, distinctions, and attributions find their final justification (and guarantee) in the statements of fact belonging to the lowest empirical level. These statements are demonstrable[14] from the mere impressions on our senses, which Quine calls stimulations and St. Thomas calls *phantasms.*

Modern idealism lends credence to the view that the identity thesis – the thesis that affirms the identity of the knower and the known – rests on a radical failure to grasp the status of subjective representations. The thesis is thus regarded as naïve, as falling prey to the arguments of the skeptics, and thus unable to provide a justification for knowledge. The identity thesis, however, is compatible with contemporary epistemology, at least as developed, for example, by Quine.[15] In the process of knowing, there is necessarily a moment when the use we make of the intelligible species leads us to a stimulatory relationship with reality. This relationship ensures the interface between the one who knows and what he knows. Consequently, wouldn't it be possible for us to say that at the moment when the stimulus is both an element of reality and an element of knowledge, at that moment they are one thing?

14 In other words, we know whether they are true or false.
15 The same is true for epistemologies that rival Quine's, such as the one developed by Plantinga. See, Alvin Plantinga, *Warrant: The Current Debate* (Oxford: Oxford University Press, 1993).

SELECTED BIBLIOGRAPHY

Texts of Aquinas

Thomas Aquinas. *Against the Averroists: On There Being Only One Intellect.* (*De unitate intellectus contra Averroistas.*) Translated by Ralph McInerny. West Lafayette, Ind.: Purdue University Press, 1993.

_____. **Disputed Questions on Truth. (De veritate.)** Translated by R. W. Mulligan, J. V. McGlynn and R. W. Schmidt. Three Volumes. Chicago: Henry Regnery, 1952–1954.

_____. *On Being and Essence.* (*De ente et essentia.*) Translated with introduction and notes by Armand Maurer. Toronto: Pontifical Institute of Mediaeval Studies, 1968.

_____. *Summa Contra Gentiles.* Translated by Anton Pegis, James Anderson, Vernon Bourke, and Charles O'Neil. Five volumes. Notre Dame, Ind.: University of Notre Dame Press, 1975.

_____. *Summa Theologica.* (*Summa theologiae.*) Translated by the Fathers of the English Dominican Province. Three volumes. New York: Benziger Brothers, 1947.

Note on the method of citing the *Summa theologiae*. The *ST* is divided into three parts, the second of which is subdivided into two further parts. Each part contains questions, which in turn are subdivided into articles, containing objections, an authoritative counter (*sed contra*), the body of the article, and responses to the objections.

The method of citation used in this book is the following: Roman numerals identify the parts, then Arabic numbers refer to the questions and articles respectively. If no other notation follows, the reference is to the body of the article. Lastly, "obj." refers to an objection, "sc" refers to the *sed contra*, and "ad" refers to the response to an objection. The parts are cited as follows:

I   First part (*prima pars*)

I-II   First part of the second part (*prima secundae*)

II-II   Second part of the second part (*secunda secundae*)

Thus, *ST* II-II 23.1 ad 3 refers to the response to the third objection in the first article of question twenty three of the second part of the second part.

Texts of Wittgenstein

Wittgenstein, Ludwig *Blue and Brown Books*. Oxford: Blackwell, 1964.

_____. *Philosophical Grammar*. Edited by Rush Rhees. Translated by Anthony Kenny. Berkeley: University of California Press, 1974.

_____. *Philosophical Investigations*. Translated by Elizabeth (G. E. M.) Anscombe. Third edition. Oxford: Blackwell, 2001.

_____. "Philosophy." Sections 86–93 (pp. 405–35) of the so-called "Big Typescript" (Catalog Number 213). In *Philosophical Occasions* 1912–1951. Edited by James Klagge and Alfred Nordmann. Cambridge: Hackett, 1993, 160–99.

_____. *Remarks on the Philosophy of Psychology*. Edited by Georg H. von Wright and Heikki Nyman. Translated by C. G. Luckhardt and M. A. E. Aue. Oxford: Blackwell, 1980.

_____. *Tractatus logico-philosophicus.* Translated by D. F. Pears and B. F. McGuinness. Introduced by Bertrand Russell. London: Routledge, 1974.

_____. *Zettel.* Edited by Elizabeth (G. E. M.) Anscombe and Georg H. von Wright. Translated by Elizabeth (G. E. M.) Anscombe. Chicago: University of Chicago Press, 1967.

Secondary Sources

Alston, William P. *The Reliability of Sense Perception.* Ithaca, N.Y.: Cornell University Press, 1993.

Anscombe, Elizabeth. Intention. Oxford: Blackwell, 1957.

_____. "The Intentionality of Sensation: a Grammatical Feature." In *Metaphysics and the Philosophy of Mind, Collected Philosophical Papers II.* Minneapolis: University of Minnesota Press, 1981, 3–20.

_____. "Modern Moral Philosophy." *Philosophy* 33 (1958): 1–19.

_____. "The Question of Linguistic Idealism." In *From Parmenides to Wittgenstein, Collected Philosophical Papers I.* Oxford: Blackwell, 1981, 112–33.

Anscombe, Elizabeth and Peter Geach. *Three Philosophers.* Oxford: Blackwell, 1973.

Antoniol, Lucie. *Lire Ryle aujourd'hui.* Bruxelles: De Boeck Université, 1993.

Aristotle. *Nicomachean Ethics.* In *The Complete Works of Aristotle.* Edited by Jonathan Barnes. Volume 2. Princeton, N.J.: Princeton University Press, 1984, 1729–1867.

_____. *Politics.* In *The Complete Works of Aristotle.* Edited by Jonathan Barnes. Volume 2. Princeton, N.J.: Princeton University Press, 1984, 1986–2129.

_____. *Topics.* In *The Complete Works of Aristotle.* Edited by Jonathan Barnes. Volume 1. Princeton, N.J.: Princeton University Press, 1984, 167–277.

Armstrong, David M. "Introspection." In *Self-Knowledge*. Edited by Quassim Cassam. Oxford: Oxford University Press, 1994, 109–17.

Arnheim, Rudolf. *Art and Visual Perception*. Berkeley: University of California Press, 1954.

_____. *Visual Thinking*. Berkeley: University of California Press, 1969.

Beyssade, Jean-Marie. *La philosophie première de Descartes*. Paris: Flammarion, 1979.

Boss, Gilbert (ed.). *La philosophie et son histoire: essais et discussions*. Zurich: Éd. du Grand Midi, 1994.

Bouveresse, Jacques. "La théorie de la proposition atomique et l'asymétrie du sujet et du prédicat: deux dogmes de la logique contemporaine?" In *Mérites et limites des méthodes logiques en philosophie*. Edited by Jules Vuillemin. Paris: Vrin, 1986, 79–119.

_____. *Langage, perception et réalité*. Nîmes: J. Chambon, 1995.

_____. *Le mythe de l'intériorité*. Paris: Éditions de Minuit, 1976.

Broadie, Alexander. *Introduction to Medieval Logic*. Oxford: Clarendon Press, 1993.

Burge, Tyler. "Cartesian Errors and the Objectivity of Perception." In *Subject, Thought, and Context*. Edited by Philip Pettit and John McDowell. Oxford: Clarendon, 1986, 117–36.

_____. "Individualism and Self-Knowledge." *Journal of Philosophy* 85 (1988): 649–63.

_____. "Individualism and the Mental." *Midwestern Studies in Philosophy* 4 (1979): 73–121.

Changeux, Jean-Pierre. *Neuronal Man: the Biology of the Mind*. New York: Pantheon Books, 1985.

Chisholm, Roderick M. *Theory of Knowledge*. Third edition. Englewood Cliffs, N.J.: Prentice-Hall, 1989.

Cometti, Jean-Pierre. *Philosopher avec Wittgenstein*. Paris: Presses Universitaires de France [PUF], 1996.

Davidson, Donald. "Knowing One's Own Mind." In *Self-Knowledge*. Edited by Qassim Cassam. Oxford: Oxford University Press, 1994, 43–64.

Descartes, René. *Oeuvres de Descartes*. Twelve volumes. Edited by Charles Adam and Paul Tannery. Paris: Vrin, 1964–1976.

Descartes, René. *The Philosophical Writings of Descartes*. Volume 1. Translated by J. Cottingham, R. Stoothoff, and D. Murdock. Cambridge: Cambridge University Press, 1985.

Descartes, René. *The Philosophical Writings of Descartes*. Volume 3. Translated by J. Cottingham, R. Stoothoff, D. Murdock, and Anthony Kenny. Cambridge: Cambridge University Press, 1991.

Descombes, Vincent. *Les institutions du sens*. Paris: Éditions de Minuit, 1996.

_____. *Objects of All Sorts: A Philosophical Grammar*. Translated by Lorna Scott-Fox and Jeremy Harding. Baltimore: Johns Hopkins University Press, 1986.

_____. *Proust, philosophie du roman*. Paris: Éditions de Minuit, 1987.

Dummett, Michael. *Truth and Other Enigmas*. Cambridge, Mass.: Harvard University Press, 1978.

Engel, Pascal. "Les croyances." In *Notions de philosophie*. Volume 2. Edited by Denis Kambouchner. Paris: Gallimard-Folio, 1995: 9–101.

_____. *Philosophie et psychologie*. Folio collection, volume 283. Paris: Gallimard, 1996.

Fitzpatrick, Patrick J. "Neoscholasticism." In *The Cambridge History of Later Medieval Philosophy*. Edited by Norman Kretzmann, Anthony Kenny, Jan Pinborg, and Eleonore Stump. Cambridge: Cambridge University Press, 1982.

Frege, Gottlob. *Translations from the Philosophical Writings of Gottlob Frege.* Edited by Peter Geach and Max Black. Oxford: Blackwell, 1952.

Geach, Peter. *God and the Soul.* London: Routledge, 1969; South Bend, Ind.: St. Augustine's Press, 2001.

_____. *Logic Matters.* Oxford: Blackwell, 1972.

_____. *Mental Acts.* London: Routledge, 1957; South Bend, Ind.: St. Augustine's Press, 2001.

_____. *Reference and Generality, an Examination of Some Medieval and Modern Theories.* Ithaca, N.Y.: Cornell University Press, 1962.

_____. "Teleological Explanation." In *Explanation.* Edited by Stephen Körner. New Haven, Conn.: Yale University Press, 1975, 76–95.

_____. *The Virtues.* Cambridge: Cambridge University Press, 1977.

Gilson, Etienne. *L'être et l'essence.* Second edition. Paris: J. Vrin, 1962.

_____. *The Christian Philosophy of St. Thomas Aquinas.* Translated by L. K. Shook. New York: Random House, 1956.

Goldman, Alvin. *Epistemology and Cognition.* Cambridge, Mass: Harvard University Press, 1986.

Grégoire, Eric. *Logique non monotones et intelligence artificielle.* Paris: Hermès, 1990.

Grimaldi, Nicolas. *L'expérience de la pensée dans la philosophie de Descartes.* Paris: Vrin, 1978.

Hare, Richard M. *The Language of Morals.* Oxford: Clarendon Press, 1952.

Harnish, Robert M. (ed.). *Basic Topics in the Philosophy of Language.* Englewood Cliffs, N.J.: Prentice-Hall, 1994.

Hooker, Michael (ed.). *Descartes, Critical and Interpretive Essays.* Baltimore: Johns Hopkins University Press, 1973.

Husserl, Edmund. *Cartesian Meditations: an Introduction to Phenomenology.* The Hague: Martinus Nijhoff Publishers, 1960.

_____. *Erste Philosophie (1923/24).* Volume 2. Husserliana volume 8. Edited by Rudolf Boehm. The Hague: Martinus Nijhoff Publishers, 1959.

_____. *Ideas Pertaining to a Pure Phenomenology and to a Phenomenological Philosophy, First Book: General Introduction to a Pure Phenomenology.* Edmund Husserl Collected Works, Volume 2. Translated by F. Kersten. The Hague: Martinus Nijhoff Publishers, 1982.

_____. *Logical Investigations.* Volume 1. Translated by J. N. Findlay. New York: Humanities Press, 1970.

Ingarden, Roman. *On the Motives Which Led Husserl to Transcendental Idealism.* Translated by Arnor Hannibalssom. The Haag: Martinus Nijhoff, 1975.

Jackson, Frank (ed.). *Conditionals.* Oxford: Oxford University Press, 1991.

Kant, Immanuel. *Critique of Pure Reason.* Cambridge: Cambridge University Press, 1998.

_____. *Groundwork of the Metaphysics of Morals.* Cambridge: Cambridge University Press, 1997.

Kenny, Anthony. *A Life in Oxford.* London: John Murray, 1997.

_____. *A Path from Rome.* Oxford: Oxford University Press, 1985.

_____. *Action, Emotion and Will.* London: Routledge, 1963.

_____. *The Anatomy of the Soul: Historical Essays in the Philosophy of Mind.* Oxford: Blackwell, 1973.

_____. *Aquinas.* Oxford: Oxford University Press, 1980.

_____. *Aquinas on Mind.* London: Routledge, 1993.

_____. "Descartes on the Will." In *Cartesian Studies.* Edited by R. J. Butler. Oxford: Blackwell, 1972, 1–31.

_____. *Frege.* London: Penguin, 1995.

_____. "From the Big Typescript to the Philosophical Grammar." In *Essays on Wittgenstein in Honor of G. H. von Wright. Acta Philosophica Fennica* 28 (1976): 41–53.

_____. *The Legacy of Wittgenstein.* Oxford: Blackwell, 1984.

_____. *The Metaphysics of Mind.* Oxford: Oxford University Press, 1989.

Kenny, Anthony, Norman Kretzmann, Jan Pinborg, and Eleonore Stump (eds.). *Cambridge History of Later Medieval Philosophy,* Cambridge: Cambridge University Press, 1982.

Körner, Stephen (ed.). *Explanation.* New Haven, Conn.: Yale University Press, 1975.

Kretzmann, Norman. "Philosophy of Mind." In *The Cambridge Companion to Aquinas.* Edited by N. Kretzmann and E. Stump. Cambridge: Cambridge University Press, 1993, 128–59.

Leibniz, Gottfried. "A Paper on 'Some Logical Difficulties.'" In *Logical Papers.* Edited, translated and introduced by G. H. R. Parkinson. Oxford: Clarendon, 1966, 115–21.

Lewis, David K. *Philosophical Papers.* Volume 1. Oxford: Oxford University Press, 1983.

Libéra, Alain (de). *La querelle des universaux de Platon à la fin du Moyen Age.* Paris: Éd. du Seuil, 1996.

Lonergan, Bernard. "The Concept of *Verbum* in the Writings of St. Thomas Aquinas." *Theological Studies* 7 (1946): 349–92.

Loux, Michael J. *The Possible and the Actual: Readings in the Metaphysics of Modality.* Ithaca, N.Y.: Cornell University Press, 1979.

MacIntyre, Alasdair. *Three Rival Versions of Moral Enquiry.* Notre Dame, Ind.: University of Notre Dame Press, 1990.

_____. *Whose Justice? Which Rationality?* Notre Dame, Ind.: University of Notre Dame Press, 1988.

Marenbon, John. *Later Medieval Philosophy*. London: Routledge and Kegan Paul, 1987.

Marlies, Mike. "Doubt, Reason and Cartesian Therapy." In *Descartes, Critical and Interpretive Essays*. Edited by Michael Hooker. Baltimore: Johns Hopkins University Press, 1973, 89–113.

McDowell, John and Philip Pettit (eds.). *Subject, Thought, and Context*. Oxford: Clarendon, 1986.

Michon, Cyril. "Asymétries: Thomas d'Aquin et Guillaume d'Occam précurseurs de Frege." *Les Études philosophiques* 3 (1996): 307–20.

Moreau, Joseph. *De la connaissance selon saint Thomas d'Aquin*. Paris: Beauchesne, 1976.

O'Callaghan, John P. *Thomist Realism and the Linguistic Turn*. Notre Dame, Ind.: University of Notre Dame, 2003.

Ogien, Ruwen. *Les causes et les raisons*. Nîmes: Éditions J. Chambon, 1995.

Panaccio, Claude. "De la reconstruction en histoire de la philosophie." In *La philosophie et son histoire: essais et discussions*. Edited by Gilbert Boss. Zurich: Édition du Grand Midi, 1994, 173–95.

_____. *Les mots, les concepts et les choses*. Paris: Vrin, 1991.

Plantinga, Alvin. *Warrant and Proper Function*. Oxford: Oxford University Press, 1993.

_____. *Warrant: The Current Debate*. Oxford: Oxford University Press, 1993.

Pouivet, Roger. *Esthétique et logique*. Liège: Mardaga, 1996.

_____. *Qu'est-ce que croire*. Paris: Vrin, 2003.

_____. "Survenances." *Critique*. Volume 51, number 575 (1995): 227–49.

Putnam, Hilary. *Mind, Language and Reality, Philosophical Papers II.* Cambridge: Cambridge University Press, 1975.

Quine, W. V. *Pursuit of Truth.* Cambridge, Mass.: Harvard University Press, 1990.

_____. *Theories and Things.* Cambridge, Mass.: Harvard University Press, 1981.

_____. *Word and Object.* Cambridge, Mass: MIT Press, 1960.

Ramsey, Frank P. *Philosophical Papers.* Edited by D. H. Mellor. Cambridge, Cambridge University Press, 1990.

Raz, Joseph (ed.). *Practical Reasoning.* Oxford: Oxford University Press, 1978.

Renan, Ernest. *The Memoirs of Ernest Renan (Souvenirs d'enfance et de jeunesse).* Translated by J. Lewis May. London: G. Bles, 1935.

Robinet, André. *Le Langage à l'age classique.* Paris: Klincksieck, 1978.

Russell, Bertrand. *Logic and Knowledge: Essays, 1901–1950.* Edited by Robert Charles Marsh. London: George Allen and Unwin, Ltd, 1956.

Ryle, Gilbert. *The Concept of Mind.* London: Hutchinson, 1949.

Sanford, David. *If P, then Q: Conditionals and the Foundations of Reasoning.* London, Routledge, 1989.

Scheffler, Israel. *In Praise of the Cognitive Emotions.* London: Routledge, 1991.

Schmitz, François. *Wittgenstein, la philosophie et les mathématiques.* Paris: PUF, 1988.

Seymour, Michel. *Pensée, langage et communauté: Une perspective anti-individualiste.* Paris: Vrin, 1994.

Sommers, Frederic T. *The Logic of Natural Language.* Oxford: Oxford University Press, 1982.

Stich, Stephen P. *From Folk Psychology to Cognitive Science.* Cambridge, Mass: MIT Press, 1983.

Strawson, Peter F. *The Bounds of Sense: An Essay on Kant's "Critique of Pure Reason."* London: Methuen, 1966.

Stump, Eleonore. "Aquinas on the Foundations of Knowledge." *Canadian Journal of Philosophy, Supplement.* 17 (1991): 125–58.

Van Steenberghen, Fernand. *Le thomisme.* The "Que sais-je" series. Paris: PUF, 1983.

Verstegen, Ian. "The Thought, Life and Influence of Rudolf Arnheim." In *Genetic, Social and General Psychological Monographs.* Volume 122. Washington, D.C.: Heldref, 1996, 197–213.

Vuillemin, Jules (ed.). *Mérites et limites des méthodes logiques en philosophie.* Paris: Vrin, 1986.

GLOSSARY

This glossary contains explanations of the medieval scholastic terms and the contemporary "scholastic" terms used in this book.

Abstractionism: Thesis according to which the mind can abstract the *forms* of things from repeated experiences that we have of these things, by means of a mechanism of inferential induction. Universal entities (expressed in general terms such as horse or man) are thus regarded as being abstracted from particular things (these horses, these men). This thesis is falsely attributed to Thomas Aquinas. It arises from a questionable reading of a text of Aristotle from the *Second Analytics* (2.19 [100a4–100b5]).

Anti-individualism: See individualism.

Belief: Belief refers here not solely to religious belief, but is taken in the broad sense as referring to our general attitudes toward our surroundings. Without questioning other meanings one can legitimately give to the term (such as referring to a psychological state), in this book belief principally designates the proposition that takes the place of p in the phrase X believes p. In this case, p is X's belief. (See Pascal Engel, "Les croyances," in *Notions de philosophie*, edited by Denis Kambouchner [Paris: Gallimard-Folio,

1995]: volume 2, pp. 9–101; and Roger Pouivet, *Qu'est-ce que croire* [Paris: Vrin, 2003].)

Composition (*compositio*)*:* The combination of a subject and a predicate to form an affirmative declarative sentence. Division (*divisio*), on the other hand, is the separation of a subject and a predicate to form a negative declarative sentence.

Disposition: *See habitus.*

Division (*divisio*): See *composition.*

esse (*intentionale/naturale*)*:* We can regard this technical sense of *esse* as signifying "to exist," provided we recognize that it does not signify the existence affirmed in statements such as "God exists" or "blindness exists." *Esse* here signifies a form's way of existing, where *form* signifies that which makes a thing be what it is. This way of being can be natural (*esse naturale*) or it can be intentional (*esse intentionale*). The *esse intentionale* is not an interior representation of an intentional object, of the thing as the object aimed at by consciousness (which is how it is portrayed within a phenomenological framework widely held today). It is a cognitive attitude, the thought of something, displayed in the ability to follow a rule or to behave in this or that way (to respond with discernment, to make the appropriate gesture, etc.). Stated in another way, the *esse intentionale* is not a mental thing, but a *disposition* to think something in a certain way and to say certain things about it.

Externalism: Externalism and internalism both concern (1) how one justifies beliefs and (2) how one understands voluntary action.

(1) An externalist theory justifies beliefs by affirming that at least some of the justifying factors are exterior to the one who has the beliefs in question. These justifying factors pertain, for example, to one's membership in a linguistic

community, even to the state of affairs in one's environment. Internalism, on the other hand, affirms that the justification for our beliefs rest solely upon an internal examination of the mental states proper to consciousness (see *individualism*), and the discrimination that the subject of consciousness (the one who knows) is able to make between mental states that guarantee the truth of a belief and those that do not guarantee it.

(2) Internalism holds that voluntary action presupposes a *volition*, viewed as an internal entity that causes the action. On the other hand, externalism affirms that although voluntary action presupposes dispositions (the capacity to undertake voluntary action) proper to the agent, it does not imply the existence of a particular internal state portrayed as a volition motivating action.

Form: This term offers a paradigmatic example of lexical confusion. It can be regarded simply as a synonym for quiddity. Historically, it comes from Plato, for whom – at least if one attributes to him a theory of forms – the form is the ideal model of all sensible realities that participate in it. Sensible things are images caused by the form, which is predicated of itself: the form of the beautiful is perfectly beautiful. Aristotle very firmly contested the notion that forms exist separately from sensible things. In his view, the form should merely be distinguished from the *matter*, from that which is informed. Bronze (matter) becomes a statue by being molded into it by means of a form. In other words, that the bronze becomes a statue is a function of a form. Thus, we could even suggest that the form be viewed as a structuring function.

habitus: The meaning of this Latin term is not entirely expressed by translating it as *habit*. It is better to employ the term *disposition*: it is a tendency to behave (speculatively or practically) in a certain way. Fragility or radioactivity are dispositions of objects. Understanding or generosity are

dispositions proper to persons. Dispositions are not entities, or even occurrences (cases) of entities. We know when
a person possesses a *disposition* because he behaves in such
a fashion that only by presupposing this disposition – only
by presupposing the exercise of a certain capacity – can we
explain that he thinks this or that or behaves in this or that
way.

Individualism: This term has multiple usages. It has meanings proper to the moral as well as the political domains,
none of which, however, are retained here. In this book,
individualism signifies the thesis that mental states (the
contents of thought) can be identified (by some internal
means) without reference to the natural and social (linguistic) environment, and can even be inscribed into a *private
language*. This thesis is posed in what could be called the
philosophy of mind; it has an epistemological counterpart,
internalism. The rejection of this thesis is *anti-individualism*.
Anti-individualism is elaborated in a philosophy of mind
which shows that to identify mental states one must examine the interactions between the mind, the world, and a
social community.

Intellect (agent intellect / possible or receptive intellect):
The *disposition* to be sensorially stimulated by one's environment (possible or receptive intellect); in other words, a
disposition to have phantasms (*phantasmata*). It is also a
disposition to understand, to make use of concepts, proper
to a being that is not only sensate but rational.

intentio: This term can be translated as intention, provided
that one does not project upon it all the phenomenological
connotations it has recently acquired. Intention can be considered in two ways: (1) as a characteristic of thought to the
extent that it is about something; (2) as a characteristic of
action to the extent that it is described in terms of beliefs
held by the agent and of ends that he pursues. The exact
relationship existing between 1 and 2 is problematic.

intensional: The term "intensional" (as opposed to "intentional") is applied to a philosophical (semantic) analysis in which what is signified by expressions such as "to mean," "to think that," or "to wish that" are regarded as complete realities. It is thus affirmed that if X thinks that Brittany is to the West of Paris, there is a Thought-of-Brittany-to-the-West-of-Paris that is the object of X's thought. Intensional is opposed to extensional. An extensional philosophical analysis seeks to show that one can give an account how the cited expressions are used, without supposing that they signify complete realities. See also *esse* and *noetic*.

Intentional/intentionality: See *esse* and *noetic*.

Internalism: See externalism.

Matter: See form.

noema: See noetic.

Noetic: A term employed to describe everything linked to the *intellect's* apprehension. When we hear or read a phrase, its intelligibility presupposes that the sounds or characters function in such a way that the phrase is understood by the intellect. This does not mean, however, that the intellect grasps the meaning of the phrase understood as an *intensional* entity, as a reality consisting of a content of thought, or what Husserl calls a *noema*, an object constituted by the intentional acts of consciousness. For Husserl, such an object, even though it doesn't constitute a separately existing reality, is no less present in the acts of consciousness directed toward it. One could argue instead, however, that the noetic apprehension of a phrase simply consists in being able to interject new phrases into a dialogue (to respond "yes" or "no" to a question such as "would you like some more tea?"), or in behaving in ways that reveal one's understanding of the phrase.

Occurrence: A relation of co-variation; the dependence of one collection of properties on another collection of properties (the referent collection). Occurrence is compatible with the non-reducibility of the occurring collection to the referring collection. The notion of occurrence is particularly useful in noetic descriptions of the relationship between mental and physical properties. Occurrence helps us avoid psychophysic dualism (dualities between mental and physical substances) as well as psychic monism (all is mind) or physical monism (all is body).

phantasm: The sensory interface between the mind and the world. The phantasm correlates to sense stimulation in a being capable of sensation and thought.

Philosophy of mind: The body of philosophical research treating issues of interest to both clinical and experimental psychology. Philosophical psychology – a much neglected field in contemporary thought, but a dominant domain for Aristotle, Aquinas, Hume, and Mill – examines commonly employed phrases in order to describe our psychological life and to describe the notions that these phrases presuppose and imply. Philosophical psychology also considers the philosophical presuppositions about the nature of the mind evident in the neurosciences, such as their implicit perspective on the relationship between mind and body. The philosophy of mind, therefore, corresponds to that part of metaphysics dedicated to the study of mental phenomenon. This meaning of the philosophy of mind should be sharply distinguished from the meaning applied to it by German idealism, where it signifies the study of Mind or Spirit, considered as a reality existing apart from the particular minds of psychological subjects, and which is viewed as having its own history and logic.

Private language: *Individualism* presupposes the possibility of a private language, whose terms would find their meaning in the interior labeling of the episodes of one's inner life. Wittgenstein shows the absurdity of this presupposition. For Kenny, "Any word purporting to be the name of something observable only by introspection, and merely causally connected with publicly observable phenomena, would have to acquire a meaning by a purely private and uncheckable performance. But if the names of the emotions acquire their meaning for us by a ceremony from which everyone else is excluded, then none of us can have any idea what anyone else means by the word. Nor can anyone know what he means by it himself; for to know the meaning of a word is to know how to use it rightly" (*The Metaphysics of Mind* [Oxford: Oxford University Press, 1989], 52).

Privatism: The belief that we can have access to the contents of consciousness either independently of language or as expressed in a private language. Consciousness would thus by itself be able to be its own object.

Quiddity: From the Latin, *quidditas*, this term signifies the essence of a thing, what makes it be what it is. For example, what makes Peter be a man, is his quiddity.

Volition: A mental event of a specific nature and regarded as being what initiates an action. Theories that speak of "volitions" regard the will as the faculty of volitions, while the volitions themselves are viewed as *intensional* philosophical notions. The perspective advanced in this book is entirely different. It regards the will instead as a *disposition* to act, and thus does not hold that there are certain mental entities or even events called volitions that cause our actions.

Will: see volition.

INDEX OF NAMES

INDEX OF SUBJECTS